Also Available

A Companion to the New Testament: The Gospels and Acts
A Companion to the New Testament: Paul and the Pauline Letters

"Written in a lucid and engaging style, Skinner's *Companion to the New Testament* brilliantly explicates how the General Epistles and Revelation reveal key characteristics of early Christian communities but also shaped their identity. It offers profound insights about the sociopolitical and theological aspects of the nine books and is simultaneously very accessible—both to the scholar and to the lay reader."

—RAJ NADELLA, Assistant Professor of New Testament,
Columbia Theological Seminary

A Companion to the New Testament
The General Letters and Revelation

Matthew L. Skinner

BAYLOR UNIVERSITY PRESS

Cover Design by Savanah Landerholm
Cover image: A fresco is pictured inside the catacomb of Priscilla in Rome, November 19, 2013. The catacomb, used for Christian burials from the late 2nd century through the 4th century, is now open to the public after years of restoration. Photograph © REUTERS/Max Rossi.

Library of Congress Cataloging-in-Publication Data

Names: Skinner, Matthew L., 1968– author.
Title: A companion to the New Testament. The general letters and Revelation / Matthew L. Skinner.
Other titles: General Letters and Revelation | Revelation
Description: Waco, Texas : Baylor University Press, [2018] | Includes bibliographical references and index.
Identifiers: LCCN 2017037385 (print) | LCCN 2017040820 (ebook) | ISBN 9781481307901 (web PDF) | ISBN 9781481307895 (ebook: Mobi/Kindle) | ISBN 9781481307888 (ePub) | ISBN 9781481307871 (pbk. : alk. paper)
Subjects: LCSH: Bible. Catholic Epistles—Criticism, interpretation, etc. | Bible. Revelation—Criticism, interpretation, etc.
Classification: LCC BS2777 (ebook) | LCC BS2777.S55 2017 (print) | DDC 227/.906—dc23

Printed in the United States of America on acid-free paper with a minimum of 30 percent recycled content.

Dedicated with love and pride
to Sam.

May you never stop learning.

Contents

Acknowledgments

Innumerable people helped me complete this three-volume companion, whether they knew they were doing so or not: encouraging friends, intelligent Bible scholars, patient family members, generous people who pored over and commented on drafts of chapters, my own teachers, and other authors whom I have never met in person. Likewise, untold experiences have prepared me to write these books, including the hours I have spent learning about the New Testament as a student in classrooms, as a reader in libraries and cafés, as a participant in scholarly research and discussions, and as a member of Christian worshiping communities.

While working on the project, however, I came to realize that the most valuable helpers have been the students I have been fortunate enough to teach over the last sixteen years. Students in classrooms, conferences, churches, and online settings have spurred me to learn about teaching the New Testament and about paying attention to how people respond to the challenges of interpreting biblical writings. As a result, I have come to a deeper appreciation of how the New Testament continues to function in people's lives—how people's ongoing efforts to engage the New Testament as a conversation partner shape their imagination about God, themselves, their neighbors, and their world. My students have influenced me through their earnest and sometimes insistent expectations that my teaching must help them wrestle intelligently with the New Testament. They want to read the New Testament well, not so they will earn academic credits or succeed in a pro forma academic requirement, but so they will be critically equipped in their quests to know what it means for them to be Christian. They expect my teaching to spark their insights about what it means for today's Christian communities to engage the Bible thoughtfully and with an eye toward articulating a contemporary faith—a generous faith that energizes their intelligence and fosters wonder while it retains lively yet adapting connections to ancient Christian communities.

Students like the ones I have described benefit from books that demonstrate the value of knowing the New Testament's contents, its history, its controversies, and its potential for contributing to theological discourse. Such books need to invite new students into the conversations and raging debates that the New Testament has provoked over the centuries. I have therefore designed these three volumes as traveling companions—resources that can assist readers in their own journeys into the New Testament. I trust the finished product exemplifies the kind of teaching that my students teach me to do.

I am grateful to belong to an academic community that takes pedagogy seriously and recognizes the value of faculty scholarship and publishing. Luther Seminary's willingness to grant me a sabbatical leave during the 2015–2016 academic year made this project possible. My gratitude extends to my faculty colleagues who took up the slack when I was away for a year.

A number of people lent their time and expertise by reading pieces of the project and helping me discover how I could make certain chapters clearer: Eric Barreto, Greg Carey, Karoline Lewis, Carey Newman, and four anonymous reviewers. Finally, without the assistance of Barbara Joyner and Betsey Skinner, I would not have been able to find the productive environments I needed to complete the work. The two of them have my deepest thanks and my love.

Introduction

The nine books at the end of the New Testament—Hebrews, the seven so-called General Letters, and Revelation—regularly suffer neglect in comparison to the New Testament's other eighteen writings. Reasons for the neglect vary. None of the nine is especially helpful to people who want to describe the emergence of early Christian theology primarily in terms of how it might align with the Gospel authors', Paul's, and Jesus' particular teachings. Textbooks have been known to classify the books as the "other" writings in the New Testament, as if anything that is not a Gospel, Acts, or a Pauline letter deserves status as "something else." Most of the books, with the notable exception of Revelation, offer few clues about where they came from and whom they originally addressed, making them less useful for interpreters who want to reconstruct the historical particularities of the earliest Christian movement. Combative suspicions and grim images of judgment and punishment appear in several of the books, making their theological rhetoric distasteful to certain readers and sometimes difficult to reconcile with other books in the New Testament. All in all, the neglect is not a new phenomenon, even though its specific causes may have changed from time to time. It is almost as old as the writings themselves. With the exception of 1 Peter and 1 John, the books appear to have struggled to gain widespread approval among churches during the second and third centuries CE. It took time for them to receive respect and authority on par with the other literary works that also became part of the New Testament.

The nine documents nevertheless remain as much a part of the New Testament as any Gospel or Pauline letter. They are not optional reading for anyone who intends to explore the New Testament library to learn what the various writings illuminate about the development of Christian communities and what the writings declare about Christian faith and life. Because of these books, the New Testament offers a much fuller, although still far from comprehensive, account of ancient believers' attempts to construct and discern a distinctively Christian theological identity. The books provide an enduring reminder of the diversity, change, vitality, and occasional struggle that defined early Christian communities' efforts to understand who they were, how they should live, and what they should expect for their future. Studying Hebrews through Revelation allows interpreters to see more about the Christian movement's early history, the theological perspectives that gave shape to the movement, and the biblical teachings and rhetoric that continue to inform modern Christians' conversations about what it means to confess and live their Christian faith.

Each of the nine books has its own message, although some of them—such as 2 Peter and Jude—reveal a connection to one another. Because they represent a modest variety of literary genres and express their messages with different imagery, rhetoric, and emphases, it is difficult and unwise to offer a general description of all of them or to treat the whole group as a distinct collection. Nevertheless, those who explore what the nine have to say, both as individual writings and together as part of the larger conversations that emerge from the New Testament, will discover that they reveal several indelible characteristics of the early churches and the New Testament as a whole. For one thing, the writings call attention to the social dynamics of Christian communities in various locales during the Christian church's first century of existence. Many of the books speak about the difficulties believers endured as they embraced a faith that could put them at variance with their neighbors and sometimes with other Christian groups. Several of the books express great concern about people who left Christian communities because of disillusionment, fatigue, conflict, or a desire to follow other teachers. Other books address themselves to what they perceive as the moral and theological slackness of communities. According to those writings, ancient believers sometimes found it easier to talk about honoring the poor and honoring Christ than to live out those virtues among their neighbors. In one way or another, all nine aim to shape the beliefs, attitudes, priorities, and behavior of Christian communities.

In addition, the books express their theological convictions in different ways, thereby providing evidence that various churches found various kinds of theological rhetoric, imagery, claims, and hopes helpful, depending on their particular values and circumstances. The New Testament does not speak in a uniform, unfluctuating voice. Hebrews offers creative commentary on Jewish Scriptures to describe Christ's majesty with reference to ancient Israel's history and ritual practices, while James appears to draw from traditions associated with Jesus' teachings, specifically traditions that appear also in Matthew and Luke. Jude approvingly cites material from highly regarded Jewish texts that never found their way into a formal scriptural canon. The book that offers the New Testament's most explicitly scathing denunciation of the Roman Empire, Revelation, resides only a few pages away from 1 Peter, a letter that urges its readers to honor the emperor and esteem certain Roman cultural mores (1 Pet 2:13–17). No one can come away from these nine contributions to the New Testament library and conclude that Christian communities in the first century all endured the same kinds of circumstances and articulated their religious identity in duplicate ways.

A Companion to Studying the New Testament as Christian Scripture

Along with the other two volumes in this series, this book offers itself as a companion to the New Testament, not a replacement or a necessary prerequisite for the New Testament. The book will be most helpful to readers who read it alongside the New Testament, for it will help them see more in the New Testament's pages, equipping them to observe and participate in the theological conversations that the biblical texts initiate. Each investigation of a given biblical writing explores the book's origins, its general contents and purposes, and a number of its more prominent or provocative theological themes. The companion aims especially to help seminarians, graduate students, and advanced undergraduates as they learn to approach the New Testament as a collection of books that emerged from particular times and places and that continue to prompt Christian communities to articulate and embody their theological convictions. Readers can successfully work their way through the companion by studying the New Testament writings in their canonical sequence or in any other order they choose.

Reading the first two volumes of the companion prior to this one will prove helpful to some readers, although doing so is not essential. The main benefit for those who read the first volume, on the Gospels and Acts, is the very general familiarity the book provides about the world in which the New Testament writings arose—a description of the basic political, religious, and social aspects of life in Roman-controlled territories during the first century. That historical information is important especially insofar as it directs attention to conspicuous characteristics of Roman society, such as the prevalence of slavery, the role of honor and shame in social interactions, and the various connections between Roman civic life and religious observances. At the same time, additional historical information beyond those basics helps interpreters situate the writings addressed in the current volume. The companion's individual treatments of Hebrews through Revelation will therefore offer additional instruction about ancient cultural realities, to the extent that such information might prove useful for making sense of individual writings. Readers who desire a more comprehensive orientation can consult the materials listed in the bibliography of Recommended Resources for Ongoing Exploration of the New Testament, which appears in identical form at the end of each of the companion's three volumes.

Likewise, those readers who have already read the second volume of this companion, on Paul and the Pauline Letters, will understand that pseudepigraphic writings—literary works that attribute themselves to someone other than their actual author—were occasionally produced in the ancient world as attempts to honor the legacy of influential and revered figures from the past. Discussions about who wrote James, 1 Peter, 2 Peter, and Jude will briefly consider the possibility that those books were not written by Jesus' original apostles or family members but are instead pseudepigraphic letters. Debates over those books' authorship are not essential pieces of understanding what the letters have to say, but readers who are curious to learn more about the creation of pseudepigraphic writings in the ancient world can benefit from learning more about the practice from the relevant chapter in the companion's second volume or from books included in the aforementioned bibliography.

Like the other parts of the companion, this volume occasionally focuses its discussion on five different interpretive foci, subjects that allow readers to venture deeper into the New Testament writings' rhetoric, messages, and social assumptions. Those foci, which are explained in greater detail in the introduction to the companion's volume on the Gospels and Acts, are the Old Testament, the Roman Empire, women in the early church's life and theology, apocalyptic theology, and the New Testament's ongoing theological relevance. Although not each of the foci applies in equal measure to every New Testament writing, the five of them allow the companion to illuminate consistency and diversity in the New Testament's efforts to speak about God and the characteristics of Christian faith. Because the foci call attention to prominent social, theological, and moral assumptions woven through the New Testament, they allow the companion to reveal more of what there is to see in the New Testament.

Finally, this volume, like the two other parts of the companion, uses the terms *Christ-followers* and *believers* to refer to the people who belonged to Christian communities during the time the New Testament books were written. Although those terms do not align with the terminology used in all New Testament writings, using them consistently allows the companion to avoid the mostly anachronistic nouns *Christians* or *Christianity.* In doing so, the companion aims to avoid confusion about the fact that it took many generations before "Christianity" took shape as a distinctive religion and before those who expressed faith in Jesus Christ came to understand themselves as a group fully differentiated from Jews and from the Judaism out of which the Christian movement gradually and sometimes painfully emerged.

1

The Letter to the Hebrews

No New Testament writing extols Jesus Christ as Hebrews does. The book radiates an especially intense fervor about Christ. It gives lavish attention to Jesus, his nature, and what he accomplished through his death. Hebrews celebrates Christ as divine—"the exact imprint of God's very being"—and devotes itself to depicting Christ as the utter fulfillment of Jewish hopes and rituals (Heb 1:3). Everything about Jesus and what he does is magnificent, according to Hebrews. Jesus brings completion and perfection to God's intentions. The book's lofty theological rhetoric grows from a nearly exclusive preoccupation with Jesus' death; his life and public ministry receive hardly any notice at all. There is relatively little mention of the Holy Spirit. Jesus gets the attention because Hebrews regards him as the "pioneer" and "source" of "so great a salvation" (Heb 2:3, 10; 5:9).

The book's towering theological vision distinguishes itself also through its peculiar way of characterizing Jesus and the salvation he makes possible. Hebrews ushers its audience into a sacrificial landscape; the author speaks frequently of priests, rituals, and the need for cleansing. The book unfolds as an extended interpretation of various scriptural texts, aiming to establish Christ as a superior priest whose own death makes possible a new, superior covenant between God and humanity. Because Christ provided himself as an obedient sacrifice in his death, Christ-followers can have assurance that they enjoy access to God and are on the road to seeing the full realization of the salvation that God has promised. The hardships believers suffer as they wait for that fullness are normal; the struggles that afflict people of faith give no reason to doubt God's ultimate reliability.

A primary purpose of Hebrews is to urge perseverance as Christ-followers journey through hardships. The extensive theological reflections on Jesus and the consequences of his death support the book's attempt to foster faith and spiritual maturity among its audience. Hebrews views faith as trust in God and confidence in the ultimate reliability of what God promises. Christ, even with his uniquely divine status, also serves as an exemplar for a waiting and trusting humanity, for he knows what it means to persist in obedience despite the travails of suffering. Even as Hebrews makes theological claims that are admittedly esoteric, it offers those ideas to its audience with an eye toward generating rather practical results, including equipping communities of faith to remain encouraged and intact.

The book's theological outlook has proved to be as controversial as it is distinctive. Hebrews insists that Jesus and his work are the fulfillment of the salvation that God has always intended for humanity, as that salvation accomplished by Christ was expressed and anticipated through the history and rituals of Israel. The author makes the argument through a complicated and nearly arcane discussion of Jewish Scriptures. What makes the book's approach controversial are the repeated assertions that Christ, as the true manifestation of God's salvation, exposes the Mosaic law and certain Jewish rituals as obsolete and ineffective shadows of true realities. Numerous Christian interpreters throughout history have therefore relied on Hebrews in characterizing Jewish practices and identity as expressions of an incomplete religion. Whether Hebrews in fact depicts Judaism as somehow inherently defective apart from Christ is an issue interpreters must consider when they explore the book's claims about Christ's superiority and the relative obsolescence of certain pillars in Jewish theological understanding.

Although Hebrews has traditionally been categorized and titled as a letter, it does not present itself as one, except in its concluding verses, where the author asks for prayers, pronounces a benediction, mentions the possibility of a future visit from Timothy and himself, and offers general greetings to his audience (Heb 13:18–25). The book reads instead like an extended sermon or a theological treatise. In fact, it refers to itself as a "word of exhortation" (Heb 13:22), an expression that also appears in Acts 13:15 to indicate a sermon. As a sermon, Hebrews seeks to do what all the other New Testament writings do: communicate theological ideas to its readers. But Hebrews is no generic sermon or treatise prepared for delivery in any and every occasion; in its original setting, it attempted to shape Christ-followers' understanding of who Jesus was and what specific benefits were theirs because of Jesus and his activity.

The Book's Origins and Ancient Audience

Hebrews discloses very little about its origins. Its author never names himself, and the book does not include clear references to specific problems or locations, other than vague references to Timothy and to "those from Italy" who greet the audience (Heb 13:23–24). Some people in the ancient world attributed the document to Paul and grouped it with the Pauline Letters, although during those same times many other readers realized that the book's literary style and theological perspective make it extremely implausible that Paul wrote it. In many ways, Hebrews stands alone in the New Testament canon; it does not belong with the writings associated with Paul, and it has historically never been classified among the so-called General Letters, the seven shorter documents that follow it in the traditional New Testament ordering. The book's syntax and rhetoric are complex and learned; Hebrews is as stylistically distinctive as it is theologically distinctive in comparison to the other New Testament writings. Whoever it was who wrote Hebrews, that person did not write any of the other books that found their way into the New Testament. The lack of a larger organizational category in which to situate Hebrews among the other New Testament books is hardly a problem. It simply underscores the reality that Hebrews, taken merely on its own terms, offers interpreters no special impulse to draw connections between it and other New Testament documents and their histories.

The word *Hebrews* does not appear in the book. The book's traditional title *To the Hebrews* was proposed by second-century believers who surmised the document originally addressed Jewish members of the early church. That judgment arose from the book's frequent references to people, rituals, imagery, and specific passages that appear in Jewish sacred writings. Because the book consistently asserts Jesus' superiority over religious practices associated with Jewish cultic life during time prior to Jesus, people in the second century assumed it had been written to dissuade Jewish Christ-followers from returning to worship in synagogues or in the Jerusalem temple, or perhaps to convince those Christ-followers to stop worshiping in those settings and to commit their energy to building up exclusively Christian communities. While the assumption of a Jewish audience is reasonable, the book's deep scriptural fluency could also have helped it speak to gentile believers. Presumably many kinds of Christ-followers could have needed, from the author's perspective, to have a better understanding of how Jesus and his accomplishments had intrinsic connections to Jewish expectations and practices and how Jesus also marked the beginning of something new or how he brought old expectations and observances to a final completion.

Very few details about the author's specific identity manifest themselves in Hebrews. He notes, however, that he was not among those who originally heard the message of salvation that "was declared at first through the Lord" Jesus but instead learned about it from others (Heb 2:3). Nowhere in the document does the author appeal to his own insights or special authority. The sermon essentially speaks on its own.

The author's exhortations to the audience offer only a slightly greater amount of information about those people's general circumstances. The sermon equips believers to persevere in their faith and endure "hostility," "trials," and "abuse" (Heb 12:1–13; 13:13). Perhaps the target audience had been the victims of persecution from their neighbors, although the book does not say much about what kind of opposition they faced or how intense or long-lasting it was. Brief mention of public abuse and plundering of possessions could refer to violent persecution or instead to less severe phenomena, such as social alienation and economic hardship from lost employment (Heb 10:32–39). Encouragements to remain faithful (e.g., Heb 4:1–11; 10:39–12:3) suggest that the author was concerned about the possibility of Christ-followers growing discouraged and perhaps giving up their confidence in God. While some of the flagging enthusiasm may have been due to the hardships people endured, the sermon also indicates that the audience had become complacent or otherwise unwilling to pursue a more mature understanding of spiritual truths (e.g., Heb 5:11–14, 6:4–6). The author's frustration with what he regards as the audience's spiritual immaturity may be exacerbated because they were apparently not new Christ-followers. Also, some people known to the author had apparently already removed themselves from regular Christian fellowship (Heb 10:25). Hebrews therefore appears to provide theological instruction and pastoral support in order to prevent existing problems from getting worse.

Uncertainties about the identity of the author and the original conditions surrounding the book make it difficult to determine when Hebrews was written. The question of the book's date connects to questions about the book's basic argument and its original purposes. To put it another way, hypotheses about why the sermon devotes so much attention to Christ's superiority over Israel's priesthood, priestly rituals, and the law influence proposals about when the book was created. If the rhetoric of Hebrews indeed aimed to convince ancient Christ-followers that they should not participate in temple-based rituals or should not revere the Jerusalem temple, then a date of composition between 55 and 70 CE makes most sense. That would mean that the book's specific references to regular sacrifices (e.g., Heb 10:1–3) indicate or allude to Jewish rituals still taking place on a regular basis in the temple when Hebrews was written.

On the other hand, passages such as Heb 10:1–3 could instead refer to sacrifices that formerly took place on a regular basis, long ago in Israel's past before even the first temple was constructed in Jerusalem during the reign of King Solomon. Moreover, Hebrews never issues a clear command to eschew the Jerusalem temple and its ceremonies. In fact, the book never mentions "the temple" at all. Instead of telling its audience to steer clear of a still-active temple, the book appears to encourage them to see all that the temple represents (or, more specifically, all that the ancient Hebrews' tabernacles represented) as functionally obsolete as a result of the new and superior things Christ has accomplished. The theological and ritualistic impulses behind the temple in Jerusalem—the original rationales for the ancient Israelites' tabernacle and priesthood—have revealed themselves to be provisional and insufficient in light of the effects of Christ's death, according to Hebrews. The book may therefore have been an attempt to dissuade believers who wondered whether additional forms of devotion, such as offering sacrifices in the temple, could breathe life into their moribund Christian faith. More likely, instead, the book's insistence that believers have access to God directly and completely through Jesus Christ, without the assistance of a special liturgical setting or priestly rituals, would have spoken powerfully to people after 70 CE, when Roman forces razed the temple. After all, certain believers at that time might have been wondering, with palpable anxiety, whether God could still be directly encountered or worshiped when the Jerusalem temple, as well as all it represented for Judaism, lay in ruins. Hebrews might have reassured those people that the recent destruction of the temple should not fuel any sense of a theological crisis or a liturgical loss.

Hebrews implies that the temple's purpose has come and gone, rendering the temple, its distinctive rituals, and their ancient cultic antecedents themselves irrelevant. If so, then the book probably originated after 70 CE. It is highly doubtful that it could have been written after 95 CE, for probably soon after that time the church leader Clement of Rome made reference to Hebrews in a letter he wrote to believers in Corinth, a letter that has become known as 1 Clement.

The difficulty in pinning down the date of the book's authorship does not seriously affect an interpreter's ability to make sense of the writer's basic argument. Reviewing the debate over the book's date and provenance nevertheless helps an interpreter imagine what kinds of audiences might have valued the sermon and what would have made its rhetoric most convincing to them in their circumstances.

Overview

Because the homiletical style of Hebrews sometimes transitions quickly between instruction and exhortation, and because the book returns to various images and comparisons at different points, it is difficult to outline the book. The circuitousness and fluidity of its design counsels against assuming that Hebrews consists of heterogeneous or self-contained arguments and themes. The book's nearly relentless focus on Jesus Christ and his trustworthiness provides the basic thematic cohesion to the multiple movements and meditations that make up the sermon.

The Son Who Manifests God and God's Salvation (Heb 1:1–2:9)

The sermon wastes no time in introducing Jesus, God's Son, as himself superior to any other being or manner through which God has communicated to humanity. Greater than the prophets and even angels, the Son participated in creation (cf. Prov 8:22–31; Wis 7:22; John 1:3; Col 1:16) and is "the exact imprint of God's very being," the one who "sustains all things by his powerful word" (Heb 1:3). Although Hebrews does not parse those stately claims, they obviously rule out any assumption that the Son is just another messenger in God's service. He is an embodied expression of God's own self (cf. John 1:1–3; Col 1:15–20; Phil 2:6). He resembles what older Jewish traditions say about Wisdom as a personified emanation of the Divine who shares an exalted status with God (e.g., Wis 7:24–26; 9:4).

A constellation of scriptural passages expresses the sermon's perspective on Christ's superior status, drawing on various kinds of Jewish Scriptures (e.g., Deut 32:43; 2 Sam 7:14; Pss 2:7; 45:6–7; 102:25–27; 104:4; 110:1). The argument put forth by the rapid scriptural catena is at least twofold: the Son's ultimate authority derives from God and far exceeds any authority that angels possess, and the Son's majesty does not represent a departure from scriptural precedents but rather constitutes the fulfillment of expectations concerning God's royal rule over all things.

Because of the Son's exalted status, the salvation he has accomplished demands serious attention. Those who neglect the message about "so great a salvation"—announced by the Son and those who witnessed him and also confirmed by "gifts of the Holy Spirit" (Heb 2:3–4)—in effect neglect the Lord of all creation. By contrast, the disclosure of this salvation has occurred in a much more earthly, accessible, and even outwardly inglorious way; "the Son" is no theological abstraction, Hebrews declares, for Jesus was made visible and lived as one "made lower than the angels" (Heb 2:9; cf. Ps 8:4–6; Heb 2:7), a human being. Through his "suffering of death," he "taste[d] death" on behalf of all people. Salvation was not worked out in an unseen and intangible heaven. Rather, "We do see Jesus" (Heb 2:9), whose glory does not exist in isolation from the real, concrete death he died.

Jesus, a Faithful and Sympathetic Sufferer (Heb 2:10–5:10)

Having moved from the heights of the Son's glory to the sermon's first mention of Jesus' corporeal "suffering" in Heb 2:9, the book turns greater attention toward Jesus' identity as a sufferer. Because Jesus was truly human, "flesh and blood," he also shared in the human experience of suffering. Somehow, "through death" Jesus' suffering "destroy[ed] the one who has the power of death, that is the devil, and free[d] those who all their lives were held in slavery by the fear of death" (Heb 2:14–15). Being human, in all the vulnerability that comes with that mortal existence, allowed Jesus to serve as "a merciful and faithful high priest" who made "a sacrifice of atonement for the sins of the people" (Heb 2:17).

The sermon highlights Jesus' fidelity to God, drawing attention to Jesus and his faithfulness as both similar to and superior to Moses and Moses' faithfulness. The connection to Moses expands into an appeal to the audience to remain faithful, so they do not become rebellious like the ancient Hebrews who traveled with Moses and consequently were barred from enjoying final rest in the promised land (cf. Num 14:1–23, 33; 20:1–13; Ps 95:8–11). The notion of perseverance and remaining faithful despite not yet having reached the full realization of God's promises occurs frequently in the book.

Jesus' sufferings make him sympathetic to human weakness; he understands what it means to have one's faith tested, yet he endured such trials without succumbing to disobedience and distrust. His suffering, Hebrews claims, allowed him to exercise obedience as a Son and made him "the source of eternal salvation for all who obey him" (Heb 5:9). He has this influence and makes salvation possible because he is "a great high priest" whose priesthood is "according to the order of Melchizedek." Melchizedek receives frequent attention in Hebrews even though he is a rather obscure figure mentioned only twice in Jewish Scriptures (Gen 14:17–20; Ps 110:4) and discussed by a small number of additional Jewish writings. Hebrews has much to say about describing Jesus Christ's identity in relation to Melchizedek, but first the sermon pauses to impress on its audience the importance of attending carefully to what they are about to learn.

An Appeal to Hear and Embrace Advanced Teaching (Heb 5:11–6:20)

The sermon chides its audience for their lack of spiritual understanding and goads them to become mature enough to receive "solid food." Those comments set the stage for what will come in Heb 7:1–10:18, identifying that material as advanced teaching and also suggesting that the author is restraining himself from delving into excessively recondite subject matter. Hebrews briefly shames the audience over their shortcomings so it might again urge them toward spiritual maturity and "completion" (which is a better translation than the NRSV's "perfection" in Heb 6:1). The sermon affirms that its audience has "tasted the heavenly gift, and have shared in the Holy Spirt" (Heb 6:4), but Hebrews expects greater diligence from them toward faithful living. They have been negligent disciples.

By summoning people to a more confident and mature faithfulness, Hebrews does more than merely fan religious enthusiasm. The book also appeals to God's own reliability, establishing a more secure theological grounding for the trust that believers might place in God and in the completeness of the salvation God provides through Christ as a great high priest. By referring to God's original promise to Abraham (e.g., Gen 12:1–3, 15:1–5), Hebrews taps into the roots of ancient Israel's dependence on God. As Genesis presents God's promises to Abraham, they depend utterly on God's fidelity; God pledges God's own self to the realization of those promises when God binds God's own self to an oath (Gen 22:15–18). The divine faithfulness that Hebrews has in mind, then, takes its bearings from the very character of God. That divine character should not be foreign to the audience, for Jesus knows God and represents God to them very well. That is because Jesus has access to God's own self, for Jesus is the one who has ministered on humanity's behalf before God. He has done this "behind the curtain" (Heb 6:19), where God's presence was said to dwell on the mercy seat in the temple and in the tabernacles that preceded it (Exod 26:31–35; Lev 16:2).

The Superiority of Christ's Priesthood, Covenant, and Sacrifice (Heb 7:1–10:18)

The sermon's explanation of Christ's superiority relies on a particular understanding of ancient Israel's cultic life, and it consistently describes Christ as the better or truer form of many elements of Judaism. Christ serves as the consummate figure and actor in God's salvation; he is the one who makes complete all of the rituals through which the Israelites of old sought to express or maintain their nearness to God. Three major claims about Christ advance the sermon's argument. Jesus outshines any other high priest. Also, his ministry forges a new covenant between God and humanity that renders the previous covenant "obsolete" (Heb 8:13), since he entered heaven directly as a mediator before God. Finally, Christ's sacrifice is effective for all time, providing an offering that allows sins to be forgiven once for all.

To establish Christ's credentials as a superior high priest, Hebrews returns to the figure of Melchizedek and the assertion that Ps 110:4 ("You are a priest forever according to the order of Melchizedek") refers unquestionably to Christ (cf. Heb 5:6, 10; 6:20). Hebrews offers a short interpretation of Gen 14:17–20, when Abram (prior to him becoming known as Abraham beginning in Gen 17:5) meets an otherwise unknown "king of Salem" who blesses him and receives a tithe from him. Hebrews sees Melchizedek as a precursor of Christ, or perhaps even a manifestation of Christ himself. According to the sermon's interpretation, Melchizedek, just like Jesus, is both a king and a priest, as indicated by the former's name ("king of righteousness") and his acts of receiving a tithe and pronouncing a blessing. The interpretation may take some liberties, for it is hardly clear that the Hebrew words *Melchizedek* and *Salem* would actually have been understood as "king of righteousness" and "peace," respectively. Even if the sermon is only engaging in wordplay or rhymes here, still Hebrews makes its point. The absence of any details about Melchizedek's background in Genesis allows the sermon to elaborate according to its own theological imagination. Hebrews characterizes him as an eternal priest, one whose priestly credentials derive not from a genealogy, as one might expect, but from some other criterion that Genesis does not specify. Because Genesis makes no reference to Melchizedek's birth or death, Hebrews imagines him as one who remains a priest for all time. He also towers over Abraham in terms of importance, for even Israel's original patriarch recognizes Melchizedek's superiority, since he offers tithes to him as a sign of deference.

As Hebrews understands it, there are important theological points to be gleaned from the respect Abraham shows to the mysterious king-priest. Abraham does not recognize the superiority of an ordinary Levitical priest, a member of "the order of Aaron," but rather the superiority of an eternal priest. God's promises to Abraham therefore rightly connect to a different kind of priesthood, and not to a priesthood whose members regularly die and have to be replaced—in other words, the descendants of Levi and Aaron. Because Jesus Christ, like Melchizedek, Scripture's original priest, serves as a priest for eternity, he possesses the ability "for all time to save those who approach God through him, since he always lives to make intercession for them" (Heb 7:25). As an eternal priest, Jesus also exists as a holy high priest who does not need to offer repeated sacrifices on behalf of himself and others. Instead, his sacrifice of his own self constituted a perfect sacrifice, effective "once for all," as Hebrews is fond of saying (Heb 7:27; 9:12, 26; 10:2, 10).

As Hebrews continues to unpack the idea of Christ as a superior and perfect high priest, it offers comments about the covenant and practices that Jesus has effectively surpassed or rendered obsolete. For one thing, Jesus now occupies a position "at the right hand of the throne of the Majesty in the heavens" (Heb 8:1) and thus does not conduct his ministry in an earthly sanctuary, such as a tabernacle or—to extend the sermon's cultic imagery—the Jerusalem temple. Hebrews denigrates the ancient Israelites' sanctuary as merely "a sketch and shadow of the heavenly" sanctuary (Heb 8:5). As a consequence of his exalted nature and his position in the presence of God, Jesus represents "a more excellent ministry" and mediates "a better covenant" between God and humanity (Heb 8:6). A lengthy citation from the prophet Jeremiah in Heb 8:8–12 reminds the audience that the idea of a "new covenant" resides in Jewish expectations and is therefore not an innovation (Jer 31:31–34). The new covenant also includes the prospect of God no longer remembering the sins of God's people.

Hebrews employs language of obsolescence to describe how the new covenant affects the old one. One of the defects of the former system, according to the sermon, derives from the repetitive nature of the rituals performed by priests in Israel's tabernacle. They offered sacrifices on a regular basis. The repetition underscores the relative ineffectiveness of sacrifices, meaning that those cultic activities point toward an ultimate time when true perfection can be achieved—a time finally "to set things right" forever. The regular sacrifices on the tabernacle's altar can purify only the "flesh" of defiled persons; they cannot cleanse one's "conscience." Hebrews does not, however, elaborate on what it sees as the distinction between those supposedly separate parts of an individual, flesh and conscience. Yet the book does associate a cleansed conscience with an ability to "worship the living God" and the gift of "the promised eternal inheritance" (Heb 9:14–15). Evidently, then, the author thinks that the regular sacrifices played no part in securing or ensuring one's inheritance from God.

The priestly activity of Christ, as one who gave his own blood, has an effectiveness that exceeds repetitive sacrifices in a tabernacle (e.g., Lev 16; Exod 25–27) or even perhaps in the Jerusalem temple. Christ dwells and mediates in a heavenly place, which Hebrews understands as vastly superior to a temporal, physical location, for an earthly location represents only a shadow of the true reality. Moreover, Christ had to suffer only once—"once for all at the end of the age to remove sin by the sacrifice of himself" (Heb 9:26). Even though that sacrificial action is completely effective, Christ has more to do. He will someday appear again to bring salvation to completion for "those who are eagerly waiting for him" (Heb 9:28; cf. Heb 10:25).

As it frequently does, Hebrews turns to scriptural citations and images to assure its audience that the newness of Christ's work and the new covenant he mediates do not deviate from what Jewish Scriptures also expect. Jesus is hardly disconnected from all that preceded him. Newness does not necessarily mean departure. God had, the sermon insists, already indicated that repeated "sacrifices and offerings" are not God's ultimate desire (Heb 10:5, citing Ps 40:6–8 as if Jesus himself spoke those words; cf. Isa 1:10–17; Hos 6:6). Therefore, Jesus accomplishes nothing less than God's established design. By bringing an end to the need to offer ongoing sacrifices, Christ accomplished God's longstanding will. According to Hebrews, Christ therefore "abolishes the first" things (Heb 10:9) since they and even the law itself were only shadowy representations of "the true form" of divine realities (Heb 10:1; cf. Col 2:17). Upon completing his sacrifice of his own self, Christ "sat down at the right hand of God," and thus he now awaits the time when the assured salvation becomes totally complete, when his enemies become a footstool for him (Heb 10:12–13, recalling, again, Ps 110:1).

An Appeal for Confident Faith (Heb 10:19–12:11)

After such abstract and occasionally winding reflections on Christ, the effects of his priestly work, and the establishment of a new covenant, the sermon turns in this section to make a relatively straightforward appeal to its audience, urging them to draw near to God with faith. One of the primary consequences of Christ's efficacious sacrifice is the possibility of proximity to God. Believers have access to God; they can "enter the sanctuary," the place where God's presence may be found, because Christ has made a way for them to travel and has cleansed their conscience. Therefore Hebrews calls people to have "confidence" and "full assurance" (Heb 10:19, 22). Understanding what Christ has accomplished through his death and his elevation to God's right hand should make believers see Christ and the new covenant as trustworthy. The certitude that characterizes this faith should also inspire a community of Christ-followers to grow in mutual love and unity. The other side of that theological coin is this: the magnitude of Christ's accomplishment should serve as a warning against any who depart from the way they should go and "willfully persist in sin" (Heb 10:26). Those who thus treat Christ's actions with contempt have "profaned the blood of the covenant" and "outraged the Spirit of grace" (Heb 10:29). Judgment awaits them (cf. Heb 2:2–3, 6:4–6, 12:15–17).

To kindle even greater confidence among the audience, the sermon recalls times when they endured struggles and opposition presumably because of the strength of the faith they had then. The assumption is that their capacity to persevere will increase if they understand their access to God and the reliability of God, as the new covenant discloses those things, and if they draw inspiration from their success in weathering earlier trials. They also can take encouragement from the examples set by various figures in Jewish Scripture, all of whom manifested faith through their ability to trust in God even when they had yet to see the fulfillment of what God had promised them.

Faith consists of more than believing in unseen realities; it involves an ability to see the word of God as the source of all that has been made. In other words, faith perceives God's word as that which animates reality and thus perpetually testifies to the existence of God's power. Faith, according to Hebrews, has demonstrated itself in the lives of many of God's people, even when the scriptural stories of their lives and deeds do not explicitly include the word *faith*. Even those spiritual forerunners whose stories came before Abraham's—Abel, Enoch, and Noah—manifested a confident faith.

Hebrews devotes considerable attention to Abraham. It detects faith in his willingness to travel and to wait for the son that God had promised him, even as the sermon conveniently neglects to mention the parts of Abraham's story in which the patriarch takes morally questionable steps on his own to ensure that his lineage will survive. Likewise, Isaac, Jacob, and Joseph—but not their wives—receive credit for keeping alive the expectation of God's promised future. Hebrews commends those men for remaining faithful to the end of their lives. They "saw and greeted" God's promises "from a distance" without ever receiving them. They were, then, "strangers and foreigners on the earth," people "seeking a homeland" (Heb 11:13–14). They lived and died as perseverant sojourners whose faith, according to the sermon, sustained their trust in God's yet-unseen promises.

Slightly revising other stories, Hebrews also attributes faith to the actions of Moses and the Hebrews who fled Egypt and took possession of the promised land. Hebrews lifts up a relatively unsung figure, Rahab (Josh 2; cf. Matt 1:5, Jas 2:25), while it also curiously lauds a character who might be better remembered for his crimes, Jephthah (Judg 11–12). It praises Barak while utterly ignoring his renowned commander, the judge and prophet Deborah (Judg 4–5). The gallery of scriptural heroes concludes with generalized mentions of people who achieved great success and others who suffered torture, incarceration, humiliation, ostracism, and violent death (cf. Heb 13:3). As people of faith, they lived still waiting to receive the promises God had issued to them through their ancestors. What Hebrews calls "faith" was their confidence in God's reliability. That faith sustained them because in their lives they ultimately "did not receive what was promised" (Heb 11:39) and thus did not arrive at the completion of God's intentions for them. As Hebrews puts it, they were not "made perfect" but remained on a patient journey for all their days (Heb 11:40).

All of those exemplars of faith constitute a "cloud of witnesses" that should motivate the sermon's audience to persevere in "the race" before them. Jesus, too, provides encouragement as faith's "pioneer and perfecter" (Heb 12:1–2). Just as an earlier part of the sermon characterized Jesus as sympathetic to believers in their sufferings, here Jesus' obedient endurance in his suffering provides a model for believers to emulate.

The book does not allow its audience to regard tribulations as cause for despair or distrust. Rather, those struggles represent, according to Heb 12:3–11, a form of "discipline" that God administers—an idea developed with reference to Prov 3:11–12. The Greek term translated "discipline" (*paideia*) is wide-ranging in its meaning; it refers to moral education and the maturity that comes from proper enculturation. "Training" is also a possible translation. Hebrews says very little about what such discipline might mean for understanding the character of God and whether the notion of an imposed discipline implies God is the source of the various hardships people inevitably face. In addition, the sermon does not go into detail about why discipline is necessary for people who already enjoy a purified conscience and access to God. Hebrews nevertheless claims that discipline provides evidence of God's relationship to believers as that of a responsible parent to a valued child. God's commitment to disciplining expresses God's desire for believers to participate in God's holiness.

Closing Exhortations, Benediction, and Conclusion (Heb 12:12–13:25)

A series of exhortations aims to influence the audience's behavior. The commands mostly deal with strengthening a group's ethos, which is consistent with the book's concerns about the audience's community becoming fractured (cf. Heb 6:4–6; 10:25; 12:15). Although the instructions have a relatively generic sense to them, their placement in the concluding movements of the sermon helps explain their purpose. Because the commands follow the sermon's string of focused appeals about faithful perseverance, they guide the audience in how to express their confidence in God in the midst of their struggles. In other words, the instructions mean to help them successfully navigate the discipline God visits upon them.

Hebrews rarely touches on the question of how its audience should relate to the wider culture, but the sermon does commend the pursuit of "peace with everyone." As for relating to God, the audience should offer thanks and worship "with reverence and awe." Such a posture of worship befits those who approach God's presence in "the city of the living God, the heavenly Jerusalem" (Heb 12:22; cf. Rev 3:12; 21:2, 10). That reference to God's dwelling strikes a contrast to Mount Sinai, where God gave the law, a dreadful location that struck fear in Moses and the Israelites (cf. Exod 19:16–24, 20:18–21; Deut 4:9–12, 5:22–25, 9:15–21). Once again Hebrews depicts the new covenant, represented by Mount Zion, as superior to the old, represented by Mount Sinai.

The sermon's final chapter offers instructions about mutuality, respect for leaders, and prayer. Commands warn against being concerned with dietary matters and urge the audience to "offer a sacrifice of praise to God" continually through Jesus (Heb 13:15). Such imperatives appear designed to steer Christ-followers away from an interest in following dietary laws or from a desire to present some kind of sacrificial offerings to God. A benediction in Heb 13:20–21 refers to God's act of bringing Jesus "back from the dead" and to "the eternal covenant." The benediction reiterates the book's focus on the need to pursue completion and to endeavor to be obedient to the divine will.

The Book's Themes and Theological Emphases

Jesus, the Great High Priest in Heaven and on Earth

Given what the Gospels disclose about Jesus, his teachings, and his background, he certainly did not come from a priestly, or Levitical, family (cf. Heb 7:14). Apart from Hebrews, no New Testament writing characterizes him explicitly as a priest. Yet Hebrews refers to him repeatedly as a high priest, even as a preeminent high priest who is eternal and royal. As a high priest in the mold of Melchizedek (Heb 5:6, 7:17; Ps 110:4), Jesus Christ demonstrates his superiority over other priests, prophets, Abraham, Moses, angels, and all that those beings represent. In depicting Christ as such a priest, Hebrews connects him to Psalm 110, presenting him as not just a liturgical functionary but as a ruler who possesses God's authority and enjoys dominance over rival powers, whether earthly or spiritual. Eventually, when the fullness of God's intentions come to pass, those powers will become subordinated like a footstool to Christ (Heb 10:13; cf. Ps 110:1). Even Hebrews itself recognizes that its description of Jesus as a high priest is esoteric (e.g., Heb 5:11), but the description remains a vital part of the book's perspective on the significance of understanding Jesus as both divine and a human being.

Obviously Hebrews means the label *high priest* as a metaphor, describing the nature of Jesus' death as a sacrifice and emphasizing the purpose of Jesus' deeds as effective mediation between humanity and God. What makes Jesus a *great* high priest (Heb 4:14) is his superior character and the quality of the sacrifice he provides. The sermon describes Jesus as a high priest who is "holy, blameless, undefiled, separated from sinners, and exalted above the heavens" (Heb 7:26). Because he is qualitatively different from any other high priest, due to his sinlessness, he makes for a more effective mediator. Ordinary high priests, being human, "are subject to weakness"; but Christ's unique status as God's Son makes it possible for God to appoint him to be a priest who "has been made perfect forever" (Heb 7:28; cf. Heb 4:15). He therefore is an unimpaired mediator.

Likewise, the sacrifice Christ gives—his very own self—constitutes an unblemished sacrifice that is superior to animal sacrifices, which Hebrews refers to as "the blood of goats and bulls" or "the ashes of a heifer" (Heb 9:13–14; cf. 9:19–21). Christ's perfect sacrifice, the sermon claims, "has perfected for all time those who are sanctified" (Heb 10:14). As Hebrews is fond of saying, Jesus' sacrifice is effective "once for all" (Heb 7:27; 9:12, 26; 10:2, 10; cf. Rom 6:10, 1 Pet 3:18). The sacrifice has done the job, and so Jesus remains an eternal mediator for people "who approach God through him, since he always lives to make intercession for them" (Heb 7:25).

The metaphor of high priest also allows Hebrews to emphasize Jesus' humanity. A high priest, after all, performs rites among human beings for the sake of human beings. Jesus does the same. Although Hebrews speaks of unseen and heavenly realities when it mentions Jesus entering "heaven itself" (Heb 9:24; cf. Heb 9:11–12) to perform his priestly function, the book also insists that Jesus participates thoroughly in the human condition. As a priest, Jesus shares in a "flesh and blood" existence with the humanity he came to assist; he is therefore like the rest of God's children "in every respect," so he can be both "merciful and faithful" in the work he does on humanity's behalf (Heb 2:14–18). Because his sacrifice required from him obedience in the throes of struggle, he is sympathetic to those who experience hardships (Heb 4:15). His obedience in facing death was hardly without anguish (Heb 5:7), therefore showing his adversities to be real and perhaps familiar to the sermon's audience. Because he came in flesh and blood, believers "see Jesus" (Heb 2:9); he is a human being and not a spiritual abstraction or a theological ideal. That means believers can take comfort from him and regard him as an exemplar for faithful living that expresses resolute trust in God.

Sacrifice, Atonement, and Jewish Rituals

Not many New Testament writings offer a sustained and explicit description of Jesus' death as a sacrifice. That theme shows itself in references to Christ's blood and suffering in 1 Peter, but it is even more prominent and direct in Hebrews (cf. passing mentions in Rom 3:25; 1 Cor 5:7; Eph 5:2; 1 John 2:2, 4:10). The sermon does not dwell on the mechanics of sacrificial acts, however. For instance, there is no discussion of why they are a necessary means of addressing the problem of sin, only repeated insistences that ordinary sacrifices cannot cleanse the conscience although Christ's sacrifice can. Christ's death also is able to "remove sin," according to Hebrews (Heb 1:3; 9:9, 14, 26; 10:22).

Most of the book's references to sacrificial rituals fashion a weak foil to Christ's superior sacrifice. What is curious about those references is that Hebrews consistently speaks about priestly activity in Israel's tabernacle; never does the sermon mention the temples that were built as permanent structures in Jerusalem. Even though Jews essentially considered the Jerusalem temple as an extension or a new expression of the cultic realities that began during the wilderness wanderings of the ancient Hebrews, still the sermon keeps its eye on much older practices, especially when it describes Jesus' acts with terms reminiscent of the Passover rituals described in Leviticus 16 (e.g., Heb 6:19–20, 9:11–12).

The point is, it is far from clear that Hebrews describes a theology of sacrifice that all first-century Jews would have recognized or embraced when the sermon says that the blood of animals brought about purification (Heb 9:13–14, 22; 13:11; cf. 10:4). Nevertheless, the book asserts that Jesus' sacrifice purifies the conscience and actually removes sin not by making people forever sinless but by nullifying the problem of sin, which has potential to trigger God's wrath (Heb 3:7–11) and prevents people from seeing and enjoying fellowship with God (Heb 12:14).

Hebrews never implies that Christ's death pays a penalty for sin or somehow soothes the wrath of a Deity who needs to see blood in order to forgive. The notion of sacrifice functions like a metaphor in Hebrews, much like the idea of Jesus as a high priest. The sermon emphasizes that Jesus was a sinless and unblemished sacrifice (e.g., Heb 4:15, 7:26, 9:14), but that detail seems more designed to emphasize that Jesus has direct access to God in the heavenly tabernacle (e.g., Heb 9:11–12, 24) than to make the dubious claim that only an undeserving victim can be worthy enough to wipe clean the slate of sinners who have incurred divine wrath. The key feature of Jesus' death, as Hebrews sees it, is precisely that it was a *death*, and so—somehow—it was the means by which Jesus brought an end to the devil's power over death (Heb 2:9, 14–15). The sermon's perspectives on atonement and salvation—even with all the legal language, priestly comparisons, and sacrificial rhetoric—still come across as more evocative than explanatory. That does not make those perspectives less potent, but it does give reason for interpreters to avoid drawing too many theological implications about the character of God or the problem of sin from the metaphor of Jesus as a sacrificial offering or victim. Interpretations of Hebrews have sometimes offered the book as support for theories about sacrificial or substitutionary atonement for sins, but the claims of those theories often distort or exceed what the sermon itself says.

The Christian Life as a Journey toward Completion and Rest

Hebrews instructs its audience about Christ's superiority and God's accessibility to believers because it intends to nourish faith and foster greater theological understanding. The book seeks to rouse an audience that, according to the sermon, had failed to grow in knowledge or had been prevented from deepening its commitment to God. The extensive theological reflections on Jesus Christ and the consequences of his death and glorification have a particularly pastoral purpose. In exhorting the audience toward spiritual maturity, Hebrews offers a vision for what Christian hope and Christian living look like. The life of faith resembles a long journey and possesses a communal character. Motivation to endure in that corporate pilgrimage derives from anticipating the completion of God's purposes: the arrival of "perfection."

Hebrews speaks of perfection as something other than, or greater than, absolute moral blamelessness or supreme ontological purity. Perfection in Hebrews refers to a state of completion; it is to arrive at the fullness of what God desires. Accordingly, Hebrews regards perfection as a goal—the end result or product of God's intentions. The sermon exhorts the audience to journey toward that perfection as they learn more about Christ, and it faults the Levitical priesthood for not being able to bring about perfection (Heb 6:1, 7:11; cf. 7:19, 10:1, 11:40). Christ, however, embodies perfection (Heb 2:10, 5:9, 7:28). His sacrifice—his death—perfects people (Heb 10:14, 12:23). Even Christ himself, although he was "without sin" and "undefiled" (Heb 4:15, 7:26), had to be perfected by God by being obedient in his sufferings (Heb 5:8–9; cf. 2:10). Hebrews does not imply that Christ was morally purified by his death; rather, in dying faithfully he arrived at the fulfillment or completion of what God intended him to do as a great high priest. As a result, Jesus brought a solution to humanity's repetitive need for finding a truly effective way to deal with sin. He therefore fulfilled God's purposes.

It is, therefore, too limiting to consider perfection in Hebrews as synonymous with blamelessness. The sermon sees perfection as more than a moral concept. It is about reaching a goal. The book recognizes that God's salvation has been accomplished through Jesus Christ, but it also acknowledges that Christ-followers continue to pine for completion, when the fullness of salvation finally comes to pass. Like the heroes of faith in Israel's history (Heb 11:39–40), believers await the full arrival of what God has promised—the perfected and completed manifestation of God's deliverance, when Christ will "save those who are eagerly waiting for him" and they will "see the Lord" (Heb 9:28, 12:14; cf. 13:21).

Believers cannot engineer their way to experience the completion of God's intentions for them. They must wait. Yet Hebrews encourages them to seek maturity and remain faithful in "the race" they run (Heb 12:1). In its relatively panoramic perspective on Israel's sacred history, the sermon likens believers to the ancient Hebrews who sought a promised land and communed with God via a portable tabernacle. The book depicts the life of faith as a journey in which believers seek the "rest" that God will provide through the gifts God has promised (e.g., Heb 4:3–11). Like Abraham, Sarah, and their offspring, believers are people "seeking a homeland" and "desir[ing] a better country, that is, a heavenly one" (Heb 11:14, 16). As if they are perpetually unsettled refugees yearning for a permanent home, such people live with a keen awareness that they have yet to arrive at what God has promised. Even though Jesus has dealt with sin, an ultimate "sabbath rest still remains for the people of God" (Heb 4:9).

To help Christ-followers navigate that state of incompletion, or imperfection, Hebrews urges them to pursue a more vigorous confidence in God. But the sermon's strategies for doing so extend beyond stern and repeated exhortations to an audience of assorted individuals. The book aims to promote community as a means of buttressing believers' faith. When it summons the audience to persevere, it sometimes uses first-person plural forms to emphasize their corporate identity (e.g., Heb 10:19–31, 13:10–16). That syntax implies that the author and other faithful witnesses exist in solidarity with the audience. The book commends mutual love and support and expresses concern about those who have removed themselves from communal fellowship or corporate worship (e.g., Heb 10:24–25, 13:1–2). The audience does not consist of a collection of individual sojourners who need to grow in faith on their own; they are a community that travels together toward the fullness God has in store for them.

Earthly Shadows, Heavenly Realities, and the Perils of Supersessionism

When Hebrews describes Christ and the new covenant, the sermon does more than assert their superiority over other forms of ritual and "the first" covenant (Heb 8:13). Hebrews also sees them as outright replacements for outmoded religious expressions that are passing away. As far as the author is concerned, the law, the tabernacle, and the priesthood are little more than temporary shadows or types that anticipated the arrival of Jesus and the new covenant. Even Jewish Scriptures seem to be largely about anticipating Christ. That kind of theological rhetoric amplifies the notion of Christ's superiority, which Hebrews is eager to promote, but it also risks introducing problematic divisions between Christian faith and its intrinsic connections to Judaism past and present.

The sermon refers to the Mosaic law as "only a shadow of the good things to come and not the true form of these realities" (Heb 10:1; cf. Col 2:17). Similarly, ancient Israel's tabernacle was "a sketch and shadow of the heavenly" sanctuary (Heb 8:5). By contrast, Christ ministers in heaven (Heb 8:1–2, 9:11–12). That language by itself is not necessarily problematic. It means to emphasize the comparative greatness and effectiveness of Christ and his work. Hebrews argues that former things anticipated a future fulfillment and that Christ is the source and agent of that fulfillment. Nor are the sermon's imagery and means of comparison unique. They reflect the influence of Platonism, currents in Hellenistic philosophy that, to put it simply, viewed the material world as a kind of shadow realm in which the true natures of things were indistinct and incomplete in comparison to the truer, ideal forms of reality. Those true forms exist in a different realm that people must perceive in their minds. The rhetoric of Hebrews does not include much that could be considered Platonic vocabulary in a technical sense, but the influence of that general worldview is on display in the sermon's efforts to distinguish between inferior shadow forms and superior heavenly realities. The author of Hebrews was hardly the only scriptural interpreter who employed Platonic ideas during the first century CE; the Jewish thinker Philo of Alexandria was a prolific author who made use of similar assumptions and interpretive methods.

However, when Hebrews refers to the earthly nature of the tabernacle and Sinaitic covenant, it goes further than asserting that those things were incomplete or were anticipatory precursors of what God would do to bring completion to God's intentions through Christ. Hebrews sees the old system that God had instituted as now "obsolete" and bound for extinction (Heb 8:13). The sermon claims that Jesus "abolishes" the first covenant to establish the second one (Heb 10:9; cf. Eph 2:15). The old covenant appears to possess no lasting value in and of itself, according to Hebrews (cf. 2 Cor 3:7). Of course, other New Testament writings proclaim Jesus Christ as one who fulfills expectations rooted in Judaism and brings something new into existence. But Hebrews goes further than most of those texts by rendering the old covenant as something that has been exposed as insignificant and therefore perhaps now essentially useless.

According to the Gospels, Jesus, who was so critical of the Jerusalem priesthood and certain interpreters of the Mosaic law, never described the law as something to be negated; in fact, he appears to have commended the law (e.g., Matt 5:17–18). Even Paul, with all of his insistence that the law is unable to bring about justification, explicitly refused to regard the law as something that is passing away or inherently flawed (e.g., Rom 7:12, 14; Gal 3:21). By contrast, in the degree to which Hebrews denigrates ancient priestly rituals and the Mosaic covenant, the book insinuates the idea that Christ is a *replacement* as much as he is a completion. The sermon makes its case for Christ too casually at the expense of Judaism. With its Platonic undercurrents and focus on Christ's supremacy, it risks leaving the impression that Christ-followers, whether they are Jewish or not, might consider Jews who do not follow Christ as practitioners of an incomplete or deficient religion, one that is concerned with shadow realities and based on impotent rituals. When Jewish ceremonies and covenants are deemed unsubstantial, as the perspective of Hebrews implies, Jewish identity can become viewed as flawed and Jewish people considered worthy of scorn in the eyes of Christ-followers. An attitude of Christian superiority over a supposedly obsolete Judaism has been a historical reality in much of Christian history. Theological claims always have consequences, and the consequences of those particular theological attitudes have been revolting.

How much blame Hebrews might deserve when Christian theologies disparage Judaism remains an open question. The sermon's argument might not have been especially scandalous among the audience that first received the book, depending on how they understood themselves in relationship to Judaism and to their Jewish neighbors who were not Christ-followers. It is difficult to deny, however, that Hebrews occasionally reads as a strong argument for construing Christian beliefs in a manner over against another set of beliefs. The sermon construes some Christian convictions as derived from esteemed and enduring Jewish theological premises, but it is not always consistent in doing so. The book's core argument has been repeatedly used—or perhaps distorted—over the centuries in Christians' attempts to define Christianity as a superior form of religion in comparison to Judaism. Some of those attempts have asserted that Christianity supplants or supersedes Judaism, effectively taking its place. The most abhorrent instances of these views have labeled Judaism a false or inherently flawed religion. Supersessionist tendencies have been a part of Christian history and theology for a long time, and Hebrews hardly constitutes the sole or dominant source of those tendencies.

Those who interpret Hebrews therefore have obligations to keep in mind that the book does not necessarily speak for the whole New Testament in its understanding of the new covenant's relationship to Moses' covenant. Other New Testament writings give grounds for contesting what Hebrews says. They offer different ways of describing completion and fulfillment. Hebrews can therefore not speak unopposed from the pages of the New Testament. But Hebrews continues to speak its particular message nevertheless. Interpretations of Hebrews that do not push back against certain assumptions about the law and Judaism risk perpetuating ways of thinking that have done much damage—damage not only to charitable Christian-Jewish relations but also to the integrity of Christian theology in and of itself. Christian theology must always take account of what it means for Jesus Christ to be a *Jewish* Messiah. It also must not neglect to consider what it means for the initial declaration of God's salvation to be rooted explicitly in the lineage of Abraham and Sarah and their mythical standing as the original Hebrews, a people persistently chosen, blessed, and loved by a trustworthy and gracious God.

2

The General Letters

The seven books arranged in a cluster from James through Jude are often called the General Letters. That label, although it is roughly as old as the New Testament itself, often invites confusion. For one thing, it is not obvious that all of these writings should be called letters. Also, the term *general* begs for greater clarification.

Each of the books, except for 1 John, presents itself in its opening sentence as a piece of correspondence sent from a church leader to a group of Christ-followers. Those six books definitely resemble letters, therefore, but it is not clear that they all originated as that type of literature. As previously discussed, a similar situation exists with Hebrews, which has been traditionally categorized as a letter but does not consistently present itself as one. Technical debates about each of the General Letters' proper genre or original purpose have their place, but they do not need to be delineated and settled before interpreters wade into the books to understand what they have to say. It does not greatly distort the picture to refer to the group of seven as "letters," even though it may be the case, as will become clear in time, that James and 2 John, to take two examples, read as very different *kinds* of letters.

The suitability of the adjective *general* requires a closer look. It derives from a Greek expression (*kath' holikos*) that gave English the word *catholic*. The General Letters are therefore sometimes called the Catholic Letters. The Greek expression behind the titles means "concerning the whole," or "universally applicable," as the word *catholic* still does. On one level, therefore, the names *General Letters* and *Catholic Letters* function roughly as synonyms. They refer to the manner in which most of the seven books speak to their audiences. Five of the letters, all but 2 John and 3 John, address themselves to undefined and possibly widespread audiences. Unlike, for example, 1 Thessalonians, the General Letters—again, except for 2 John and 3 John—do not explicitly direct themselves to particular, defined communities or congregations in specific cities or regions. They therefore can be said to speak to all believers *generally*—in other words, to the church *catholic*—without clear regard to many distinguishing features or circumstances among specific groups of ancient Christ-followers.

At the same time, however, too much focus on the letters'—or on five of the letters'—putatively *general* scope and means of address has sometimes spawned dismissive attitudes toward the General Letters as a group, as if they all somehow lack some essential feature that makes other letters, such as those attributed to Paul and directed to specifically identified congregations, more weighty. The General Letters' traditional label has often not served them well whenever "general" somehow comes to imply "unremarkable." Preoccupation with the books' widespread, general, or catholic scope should not create an impression that they are thin or diffuse and therefore deficient.

It must be emphasized, therefore, that the books' position near the end of the New Testament and the traditional moniker *General Letters* must not encourage prejudice against them or suggest that they are flat or colorless documents. Nor does the broad scope of the audiences they address mean that the distinct circumstances of their origins are completely undetectable. Nor do they lack diversity. Nor are the letters necessarily of lesser or less specific value than other New Testament writings. Each one of them has its own message to communicate. Taken together, these seven neighbors in the New Testament library illustrate different theological perspectives and leadership values that arose in a number of distinctive Christian communities. The specific distinctions about those communities are harder to ascertain than, for example, the fractures among the Corinthian believers that Paul criticizes in 1 Corinthians, but the distinctions are there nevertheless. Like all the other New Testament writings, the General Letters add detail to an overall sketch of how Christ-followers worked out their self-identity and theological commitments in different venues during the churches' earliest decades. Like any of the New Testament writings, whether written to an identifiable small group or to a broader horizon of readers, they have the capacity to continue speaking to readers in broadly applicable, unrestricted ways.

It deserves mentioning that the General Letters share similarities with Hebrews because it is also not addressed to a specific or identifiable audience. Hebrews nevertheless was never classified with the seven General Letters in antiquity. As mentioned, some, but hardly all, interpreters during the first centuries of the Christian church were eager to group Hebrews with the Pauline Letters and even to claim Paul as the author of Hebrews. That kept Hebrews in a different category, so to speak, throughout the early church's history. In addition, because Hebrews is an anonymous document, it has always differed from the General Letters insofar as they have been traditionally associated with Jesus' disciples (Peter and John) and family members (James and Jude). Now that virtually no one argues credibly that Paul wrote Hebrews and there are debates over who actually wrote the seven General Letters, the benefit of maintaining a firm distinction between Hebrews and the General Letters has diminished for many interpreters. This companion, following the long-running precedent, treats Hebrews separately. That decision ought not obscure the fact that the label *General Letters* is useful mostly for identifying a commonality among seven books and the history of their interpretation; it is not about drawing thick boundaries around them.

In the following chapters, this companion explores most of the General Letters as independent books while acknowledging that three of them, the so-called Johannine Letters, share an especially close relationship in terms of their style, their theology, and probably their origins. It should be noted, however, that other Christian interpreters see a warrant for treating these seven books in a more integrated fashion, as a sevenfold collection that expresses a relatively coherent outlook on Christian faith and the church. Those interpreters regard the books, having been deliberately collected together in the third and fourth centuries to form what would become a vital unit within the New Testament, as corporately capable of articulating a unified theological perspective. That particular assessment of the General Letters interprets them as distinctively "catholic" or universally relevant in an additional way: in terms of how they might function collectively in the Christian communities that read them. The view assumes that one purpose or consequence of the seven letters' inclusion in the New

Testament canon in the first place was to have a catholicizing effect for the whole Christian church through history. In other words, together the books might have promoted a unifying influence within the overall (catholic) Christian church, its Scriptures, and its theology.

Whether interpreters eventually choose to ascribe a *collective* purpose or a catholicizing impulse inherent in—or emerging from—the seven General Letters as a group or not, an introductory exploration into the books proceeds best by calling attention to their individuality. Interpreters can then explore further and decide for themselves whether a warrant exists for identifying a collective purpose in the letters together. Understanding what each of the letters says on its own is the primary task, especially since the letters' particular voices and theological rhetoric vary so noticeably. Aside from the very similar features and outlook that give cohesion to 1 John, 2 John, and 3 John, the seven writings show considerable variation in their style and syntax. They represent the work of at least five different authors. Each book has its own literary tendencies and its own messages to communicate. Each expresses its own hopes and its own concerns, even though multiple books may address a given issue in similar ways. In fact, the author of 2 Peter evidently drew some of the letter's material and rhetorical strategy from Jude. A few common themes appear in all of the letters as well. For example, each one urges believers to conduct themselves with appropriate morality and to guard the unity and vitality of their communities by resisting false teachers, misguided teachings, or anything else that might lure Christ-followers toward error or complacency.

Interpreters do not agree about who wrote the various General Letters. The three Johannine Letters are essentially anonymous, although ancient believers associated them with the Gospel according to John. The other four letters claim to come from various writers, but it is possible that some or all of them are pseudepigraphic writings. Debates about authorship differ, depending on the document in question. As with the disputed Pauline Letters, and as explained in the second volume of this companion, each book and each authorship debate must be considered on its own. For example, a very strong case can be made that 2 Peter is pseudepigraphic, but no one can declare a conclusion about the authorship of James without relying on a heavy measure of speculation. The point of discussing the authorship of the General Letters is not to settle those questions as a precondition to studying the books themselves. Instead, exploring questions about a given writing's origins should be considered as a piece of digging deeply into what the letter has to say and how it constructs its argument to its audiences. Interpretation of a letter can go forward while interpreters remain undecided or even forever indifferent about the true identity of that letter's author.

Together the General Letters reiterate what the rest of the New Testament also reveals: the first century of the Christian church's existence was a time of, among other things, lively theological discovery and debate, vital attempts at self-definition while navigating through change and occasional social pressures, and intense effort to maintain cohesive Christian communities that sometimes seemed in danger of falling apart or losing their way. As voices still speaking from that energetic history, the letters offer a modest range of perspectives that derive from different pockets of the early church. The letters appear to come from different times over a relatively wide span of decades. Individually, they give evidence of various Christian communities in different places trying to articulate their particular visions for what it meant to live as Christ-followers. All of the letters certainly share at least this aspect in common: these writings endeavor to equip Christian groups to persist in faithful living, even as various circumstances threatened to make it difficult for churches to do so.

3

The Letter of James

James shows a pronounced fondness for moral exhortation. The letter expresses great interest in how Christ-followers conduct themselves. Because James refers explicitly to Jesus only a few times and to the Holy Spirit perhaps once, and because it does not corroborate its moral teachings with obvious appeals to Jesus' incarnation or his death, some interpreters have hastily disparaged James as lacking theological sophistication. The book's detractors see its moral concerns as poor substitutes for meatier theological teaching. Also, because James offers a description of Christian salvation that evidently seeks to counter an understanding of justification that was associated—accurately or not—with the apostle Paul, people often treat the book as a weak foil to Paul and to Paul's ways of constructing a theological argument.

Against those who would hastily denigrate James as not theological enough: the quality of a book's theology cannot be evaluated by its rhetorical affinities with Paul's writings and by the number of times it says the words *God* or *Jesus Christ.* James may not quote Jesus' sayings directly, but in several places its statements resonate very closely with material Jesus speaks in the Synoptic Gospels. Furthermore, the clarification James seeks to provide regarding the nature of justification is hardly interested in engaging in abstract debates about the mechanics of salvation. James would rather discuss what theology looks like when lived. The letter's distinctive outlook on God and faith recognizes that Christian theology, a theology rooted in Jesus Christ, is a theology of agency and action, for people's theology inevitably expresses itself in people's conduct. That conduct, moreover, has tangible outcomes for the well-being of other people, especially vulnerable people. Conduct, like the theology that drives it, can build up or tear down.

Theology, for James, therefore has more to do with how one lives than with how one defines or arranges theological concepts. Accordingly, James offers its own particular way of instructing its readers about the manner of Christian living, and the letter does so with a passionate desire to steer its audience away from shallow, complacent faith and toward a new quality of life that God makes possible. James sets its eye on describing the visible and tangible qualities of true religion (cf. Jas 1:27).

The Letter's Origins and Ancient Audience

It is extremely difficult to reconstruct the historical context surrounding James—who wrote it, when, and for whom it was written. James reveals very few specific details about its target audience and about exactly how the letter expects to influence an audience living in particular circumstances. The letter's first verse directs the document to "the twelve tribes in the Dispersion," which might indicate Jewish Christ-followers living anywhere in the Roman Empire. Even so, the reference to a dozen dispersed "tribes" need not specify an exclusively Jewish group of readers. More probably the expression identifies all believers, whether Jewish or gentile, as a new expression or an outgrowth of ancient Israel, characterizing Christ-followers as a currently displaced but nevertheless set-apart community inhabiting a foreign world (cf. 1 Pet 1:1–2, 2:9–12). The letter also contains numerous echoes to a wide range of Jewish Scriptures, including portions of the Torah, the Prophets, Psalms, and wisdom literature. Those scriptural allusions could indicate an audience, whether Jewish or gentile, with a vibrant fluency in Jewish tradition and identity.

The letter refers to its audience as a collection of people who interact with one another in commercial and worship settings. When the community gathers, it is, according to James, called either a "synagogue" (rendered as "assembly" by the NRSV in Jas 2:2) or a "church" with designated "elders" (Jas 5:14). Whoever first read the letter would have been familiar with meeting corporately with other believers for worship and fellowship; the letter's vision for the church sees it as a cooperative community and not a collection of isolated individuals.

The letter seeks to help church communities become—or remain—hospitable in several ways. It speaks against boasting and selfishness. It warns about "the tongue" as a small thing capable of doing great damage to other people. It speaks most frequently and most memorably about the charity and dignity that poor people deserve and about the judgment that will befall those who hoard their wealth and power at the expense of others. The specific rhetoric used when James considers poverty and wealth suggests the letter's primary audience was neither especially poor nor especially wealthy, for the primary focus falls on the proper ways for a Christian community to regard and treat both poor and rich people. In developing that focus, James speaks about the very poor and the very rich as if they were outside groups. The letter criticizes those who baldly belittle their poor neighbors by giving preferential treatment to their wealthy ones. It also criticizes those who fail to meet the poor's conspicuous needs. The intended recipients of James probably represented a modest range of socioeconomic statuses.

Much of the moral exhortation in James gravitates toward a core theological assertion: authentic belief expresses itself in how individuals and a community of faith conduct themselves. One stark expression of this idea asserts, "A person is justified by works and not by faith alone" (Jas 2:24). That statement appears to be a reaction against the theology associated with Paul, who claimed that "a person is justified by faith apart from works prescribed by the law" (Rom 3:28; cf. Gal 2:16). The letter's audience may therefore have had some familiarity with that theology, with slogans meant to summarize it, or with other people's attempts to exploit it for their own ends. It does not follow, however, that the original readers of James had had direct contact with Paul, his writings, or any of his associates. At the least, James assumes its original audiences were not utterly isolated from other believers or from Christian ideas that were making the rounds.

The Question of Authorship

The author identifies himself as "James," a name that could also be translated "Jacob." Apart from the name *James* in the opening verse, no other part of the letter refers to this person. James was a popular name, and other New Testament writings refer to more than one man known by it. Throughout the church's history, however, traditions have identified the "James" of this letter as the brother or half-brother of Jesus, who for a time led the church in Jerusalem (Acts 12:17; 15:13; 21:18; Gal 1:19; 2:9, 12; Jude 1) prior to his execution, which occurred in 62 CE, according to the Jewish historian Josephus.

Interpreters sometimes express skepticism about whether Jesus' brother or half-brother could have really written this letter. The relatively sophisticated quality of the book's Greek fuels doubts about whether someone from rural Galilee could have attained such literary skill. In addition, the book was slow to gain widespread acceptance during the first few centuries of the church's existence, evidently because several influential leaders during those centuries likewise expressed reservations about the possibility that one of Jesus' relatives was really the book's author. Some interpreters label the book an assorted collection of Christian wisdom traditions and associate its ethical accents and vocabulary with materials and movements from the early second century, which would place the letter's composition well past the life span of Jesus' siblings. Those who propose, for whatever reasons, that James is a pseudepigraphic letter cannot strengthen or weaken their case by considering the author's style and theology alongside other documents, because there are no existing writings from Jesus' sibling James to which this letter can be compared.

Despite the doubts and debates, the identity of the actual author proves essentially unimportant to the book's arguments since the letter never explicitly appeals to James the brother of Jesus, his privileged knowledge, or his experiences. As a contrast, the Pastoral Letters, which are almost certainly pseudepigraphic documents, rely on a kind of literary fiction about Pauline authorship to reinforce their message about the importance of imitating Paul and embodying his distinctive legacy. Yet, as far as the Letter of James is concerned, the document's message does not rest on anyone's particular authority or specific insights. James presents a theological argument that stands or falls on what it says, not on the prominence or expertise of the person who wrote it.

In sum, nothing in James itself can confirm or deny who the book's author was; nor does the book clarify from where or to whom it was written. Proposals about the authorship of James remain widely varied and deeply speculative. While this situation frustrates certain historians, in the end it does not have a terribly weighty effect on how one understands the message of the book. Answers to the authorship question will not finally contribute much toward making James' contributions either more or less understandable or more or less compelling.

The authorship question connects to the challenge of determining when James was written and therefore exactly what kinds of circumstances it might address. Some interpreters weigh the various proposals and date the book early with relation to the rest of the New Testament, perhaps as early as 50 CE, which would make it slightly older than even 1 Thessalonians. Those views tend to be influenced by the assumption that the book's plausible author was indeed Jesus' brother and by the specious judgment that James misunderstands Paul's understanding of justification. Other interpreters place the book in the first decade of the second century, but this dating tends to be influenced by the conviction that James can best be described as a series of disconnected proverbial sayings. If James is that kind of literature, the reasoning often goes, then it can be lumped together with other movements in early second-century Greco-Roman moral instruction. When James is considered to have been written that late, the book's theology appears even more distant from Paul's, making the letter's theology appear less ancient and thus perhaps easier for some to dismiss as a deviation from Paul's supposedly more original ideas. In the end, however, all the options for authorship and dating remain possible but indistinct. It nevertheless seems most plausible to date the letter after a time when teachings associated with Paul would have gained relatively widespread traction and popularity, which still could have been anytime between 50 and 75 CE. The author of James engages Pauline teachings, as will be discussed shortly, but not necessarily at a great temporal distance from Paul's letters or as one hampered by an inability to understand Paul.

Overview

James introduces itself as a letter to a dispersed audience and proceeds to deliver what looks instead like a general treatise on the kind of conduct that is appropriate to Christian faith. The book's tendency to speak in generalizations does not disqualify it from being a letter, however. It is a letter with its own particular concerns and distinctive theological rhetoric.

With all of James' exhortations and admonitions, it occasionally moves quickly from one idea to the next, sometimes returning to themes introduced previously. These qualities make it difficult for an overview to trace an underlying argument or specific purpose in the document, but they do not mean the letter proceeds haphazardly. The handful of themes that recur throughout several of the letter's short discussions gives James its particular rhetorical force. The one idea that does perhaps the most to hold the whole book together is the conviction that authentic Christian living manifests the same active generosity that God displays, for the mercy that believers expect to receive one day from God should characterize their conduct now.

Exhortations concerning Endurance, Wisdom, and Obedience (Jas 1)

At least three themes weave themselves through the opening paragraphs of James. The letter commends the first of these, endurance, as a characteristic of maturity and as something forged by the "trials" believers endure. A trial, or "temptation" as the NRSV translates the same Greek word (Jas 1:2, 12–14), tests a person, revealing a person's true character and perhaps strengthening it through challenge or adversity. James avoids describing specific trials in detail, but the context suggests that these tests have to do with the human inclination to sin or with the weakness of people's self-control in the face of their desires, which was a familiar theme in Greco-Roman moralistic instruction. The trials James has in mind pose threats to a Christ-follower, for they do not come from God. James nevertheless builds confidence for a person's ability to endure such threats, for the letter declares that trials offer opportunities for growth.

Temptation does not come from God, but wisdom—another important theme in James—certainly does (cf. Prov 2:6–7). Influenced by motifs, emphases, and theological foundations associated with divinely ordained wisdom in books such as Proverbs and Sirach (a Jewish writing also called Ecclesiasticus), James speaks of God's wisdom, here and later in the letter, in terms of its durability and its relationship to God's righteousness. This wisdom, as a gift from God, produces moral purity and helps believers guard themselves from evil and contentious behavior.

If trials produce endurance that builds character, and if wisdom guides character, obedience is a manifestation of that character. James insists that "doers of the word" are people who know who they are and who act consistently with their identity. Believers pursue obedience, which is the third of the letter's key themes appearing in the first paragraphs, but not to appease God or to express gratitude in return for God's gifts. Rather, obedience expresses believers' new existence as people born "by the word of truth." James sharply criticizes those who are "double-minded": just as God is "the Father of lights" without shadow, God's people either express faith or they do not. James allows little room for a middle ground. Because Christ-followers know God's "perfect law, the law of liberty" (Jas 1:25; cf. Jas 2:8–12; Matt 22:39; Mark 12:31; Luke 10:27; Rom 13:9; Gal 5:14), they inevitably must align themselves with God. Doing so means behaving differently from those whose wickedness and anger pollute the world, and acting with a singular devotion to God instead.

Active Faith (Jas 2)

The letter's focus on obedience continues into this section and grows in intensity as James argues that having faith in Christ necessarily expresses itself in good conduct toward others. A brief illustration about giving preferential treatment to the wealthy and powerful at the expense of the poor and disadvantaged provides a stark lesson about what this obedience looks like in action. Showing partiality to the wealthy exceeds rudeness, for it contradicts God's express concern for those who are poor. When believers, no matter what their own social ranks, fail to welcome and honor the poor or to care for their basic needs, they shame the very people who are "heirs" of God's kingdom (Jas 2:5).

James boldly asserts that "faith apart from works is barren" and also even "dead" (Jas 2:20, 26), implying that believers who oppress those whom God favors, the poor, reveal themselves to be double-minded and inconsistent at their core. To support those assertions, Jas 2:20–24 turns to Abraham, the same exemplar of faith Paul highlights in Romans 4 and Galatians 3. Abraham's willingness to sacrifice Isaac demonstrated his faith, says James. In Abraham's case, "Faith was active along with his works, and faith was brought to completion by the works." James also highlights Rahab, the woman who protected and even reassured Hebrew spies when they came to Jericho (Josh 2; cf. Heb 11:31). She, too, provides an example of a person in Scripture whose works confirmed her faith; by her works, she fully manifested her justification.

Cautions about Speech and Its Potential to Destroy (Jas 3:1–12)

Various metaphors describe the power of words and of those who can successfully master their speech. The tongue is a small thing, but it has outsized influence, like a horse's bridle, a ship's rudder, and a single flame that produces a forest fire. Because of words' capacity to cause harm and humanity's inability to "tame the tongue," the letter cautions that few people should offer themselves as teachers. What a teacher says has significant influence over others—what they will believe and how they will act. Because teachers can lead others astray, they can expect to face a more demanding judgment.

Even as James laments people's inability to keep their words from doing damage to other people, who are "made in the likeness of God" (Jas 3:9; cf. Gen 1:26), still the book does not allow teachers or anyone else to resign themselves to inaction when it comes to controlling their speech. Just as double-mindedness received scorn earlier in the letter, criticism here falls on those who are double-tongued. The letter decries the inconsistency of a blessing and a curse emanating from the same mouth, and so James infers that one's speech reveals one's true nature. The implication is that believers must actively devote themselves to self-control in using their tongues to build up and not tear down one another.

The Character Produced by God's Wisdom (Jas 3:13–5:6)

Explicit references to wisdom return to the letter at the beginning of this section. Just as Jewish wisdom traditions set wisdom and foolishness in opposition (e.g., Prov 9), James contrasts wisdom "from above" with false wisdom that is "earthly, unspiritual, devilish" (Jas 3:15). True wisdom manifests itself in activity that avoids partiality and promotes healthy relationships that exemplify God's expressions of peace and mercy.

Having established divine wisdom as the source of believers' "good fruits," the letter exhorts its audience about a number of subjects. James takes aim at those who are contentious, covetous, arrogant, slanderous, and presumptuous. The most scathing language directs itself toward the rich, for they have hoarded resources, reserved wealth and luxuries for themselves, and preserved their advantages by perpetrating injustice against their own "laborers" and "harvesters," whom they defraud.

James indicts the wealthy for condemning and murdering "the righteous one" (Jas 5:6), an accusation that refers not particularly to Jesus' death but generally to powerful people's willingness to manipulate legal systems and privileges to their advantage. Those power plays destroy innocent lives, and they perpetuate poverty and injustice against the vulnerable people who are dear to God (cf. Jas 2:6). James' biting statements serve as warnings to those in the letter's audience who might be tempted to imitate those rapacious behaviors or to give undue honor to their elite neighbors. The statements also reaffirm God's special regard for the poor (cf. Jas 2:5).

Even though this section of the letter does not mention Jesus by name, many of its admonitions nevertheless resemble the themes and tenor of Jesus' teachings as recorded in the Synoptic Gospels and especially in material associated with Q, the probable source of many of Jesus' sayings in Matthew and Luke. Examples include encouragements to ask God for what one needs (Jas 4:2c–3; cf. Matt 7:7–8, Luke 11:9–10), warnings about making plans without considering the transitory nature of life (Jas 4:13–15; cf. Luke 12:16–21), and woes pronounced against the rich (Jas 5:1; cf. Luke 6:24). The promise of a coming judgment also winds its way through this section, as well as other parts of the letter, even though James does not develop any explicit connection between divine judgment and Jesus' return.

A Community of Patience and Healing (Jas 5:7–20)

The simple command *be patient, therefore*, which begins this final section, appears to proceed from all that comes before it—the entire letter thus far. All aspects of the Christian life lived in anticipation of Jesus' "coming," his *parousia* in Greek, rightly assume the character of patient waiting. This lifestyle exhibits a confident and unhurried expectation of God's promises, pursues peace with others, endures suffering, values personal integrity and honesty, and engages God in both prayer and song. No one who reads the whole of James can mistake its notion of a life marked by Christian patience for a call to disengaged passivity.

Most of the imperatives in James are plural in form, issuing commands and encouragements to people collectively. In the letter's concluding sentences, James becomes even clearer about the fact that all along it has been addressing communities and not disconnected individuals. The final sentences speak of prayers and rituals performed on behalf of sick people in a corporate setting, and James affirms the importance of mutual confession and supplication among a congregation's members. The letter commends those who seek out and bring back people who stray from the community and its core beliefs, promising that such acts of correction and compassion "cover a multitude of sins." The faithfulness, self-discipline, patience, and active solidarity that James demands from people may sound arduous for individuals, but a community that works together to embody those characteristics and to make up for whatever some members might lack in certain dimensions of character and maturity appears to reflect what James has in mind.

The Letter's Themes and Theological Emphases

Justification by Works

The author of James likely had some familiarity with the kinds of arguments Paul advanced concerning Abraham's importance for understanding justification, for those types of arguments appear nowhere else in the New Testament except Romans, Galatians, and Jas 2:14–26. The letter's sharp distinction between faith and works also suggests that it aims to be in dialogue with theological ideas associated with Paul, offering a response or clarification of some kind. The similarities appear to be too pronounced to be the result of pure coincidence.

It does not follow from this basic proposal, however, that James sets itself up as a direct rebuttal to Paul in particular or to specific letters Paul wrote. Paul's convictions about faith and justification could have been in circulation before he wrote his letters, perhaps even proposed by other, unknown Christian teachers. James also does not present Paul's ideas about justification with strict accuracy: Paul never wrote that "a person is justified . . . by faith *alone*" (Jas 2:24, emphasis added). Moreover, Paul also maintained that faith produces consequences in one's behavior; his letters frequently discuss the kind of life and activity that should inevitably proceed from authentic faith. James may therefore reflect a misunderstanding of Pauline ideas. This means that the author of James might have been the one who was confused about Paul's teachings, but more likely it means that the letter tries to correct believers or other teachers who have misarticulated or misapplied the Pauline concept of justification by faith, as if that theological principle somehow promotes or excuses a disregard for ethical and charitable living among believers.

If there are pronounced differences between how Paul's letters and James view the role of faith and works with regard to justification, those differences lie mostly in what the respective authors mean by the words *faith* and *works*. For its part, James speaks about *faith* and *belief* (which are both legitimate translations of the same Greek word) as acts of professing or affirming. That kind of faith involves statements of loyalty to Christ and trust in what God does because of Christ. In Paul's letters, by contrast, faith refers to living in union with Christ, fully participating with him in the new realities God is bringing into being through the gospel. A Pauline notion of faith includes almost by definition a new way of living, one that expresses a person's unity with Christ. As for works, when James refers to them, the letter has in mind acts of mercy or the "good fruits" that correspond to God-given wisdom (Jas 3:13–17). By contrast, the works that play no part in God's justifying activity according to Romans and Galatians are explicitly "works of the law," for God does not justify people through the power of torah (e.g., Rom 3:20, 28; Gal 2:16; 3:10). Paul does, however, indicate his high regard for the works Christ-followers perform to express the new life that is theirs through faith (e.g., Rom 12:1–2; 13:8; Gal 5:6; 6:10; 1 Thess 1:3). James and the Pauline Letters therefore appear in some measure to be talking about different dimensions of a particular theological question. They are not necessarily in direct conflict about the key details of that question, even though they approach the matter from separate angles.

Comparing James to some of Paul's letters illustrates that different New Testament writings often approach related ideas from different directions and with different nuance. The books operate with their own assumptions about terminology and the contexts in which Christ-followers express their theological understanding. There are subtle differences between James and Paul, but those differences have themselves been misconstrued and thus magnified in unwarranted ways from time to time in the church's history. Interpreters miss the point if they think about this particular intracanonical difference as either an insignificant instance of quibbling over fine points or a winner-take-all contest to assert ideological purity.

For James the issue concerning justification appears to be less about opposing Pauline ideas or slogans and more about ensuring that Christ-followers do not stray far from their Christ. The argument in Jas

2:14–26 must be considered in light of the letter's wider context, especially James' unmistakable concern for those who are poor. Many of the specific works James commends are deeds that show hospitality and mercy toward people who suffer and who lack social status. If Christ-followers assume that merely expressing loyalty to Jesus exempts them from true, hospitable solidarity with the poor and vulnerable members of society, James tells them they are thoroughly wrong. James pursues the question with such seriousness—pronouncing "faith without works" as "dead" in Jas 2:26—because the book contends that the poor will suffer most of all if Christian faith, however one defines it, manifests itself only as a system of beliefs or a perfunctory theological pledge of allegiance. James refuses to accept a faith that does not inspire believers to seek their disadvantaged neighbors' well-being. After all, it is precisely "the poor in the world" whom God has favored (Jas 2:5).

The Muted Theology of James

James has sometimes suffered neglect from Christian interpreters who minimize the book's value because it has little to say in explicit terms about Jesus Christ. The letter's moral exhortations proceed out of rather general claims concerning God's graciousness and the certainty of divine judgment, not from especially definitive statements about Christ's example or what Christ accomplished through his death and resurrection. But those generalities should not be taken as grounds to conclude that James lacks theological vitality. James' theology comes through in the book's pastoral rhetoric, especially when James refers to God's wisdom and subtly recalls memories of Jesus' teachings. Fed by those theological undercurrents, James proceeds to promote a vision for Christian living that flows from the author's understanding of who God is, what God has revealed, and what God provides. Because the book makes its arguments in ways that are rather different from the approaches of other New Testament writings, James demands from interpreters a different kind of attentiveness and listening than some other books require.

James tells its readers that Christian communities are obligated to consider what kind of living best manifests their identity as Christ-followers, and then they are obligated and empowered to live that way. James may not offer a detailed road map to solving the problems posed by evil, poverty, and dissension, but its exhortations consistently come with an eye focused on the importance of believers' character. Mature Christian faith devotes itself to addressing trials with character molded by conviction, mercy, and generosity. That character comes from God and aligns with God's expressed desires for human flourishing.

Particularly because of the outrage James directs toward injustices suffered by those who are poor, and because of James' expectation that God is committed to address those indignities and moral crimes, James has fed the imagination of liberation theologies over the last half century or more. Comments about God having "chosen the poor in the world to be rich in faith and to be heirs of the kingdom" (Jas 2:5; cf. 4:6) reaffirm other biblical material to support the familiar notion that God has clearly demonstrated a "preferential option for the poor." James directs the church's attention toward the vulnerable people in and around a community of faith while urging Christ-followers to renounce the abuses perpetrated by oppressors and to offer life-giving charity. The reverberations of Jesus' own history, including his teachings and his downfall alike, cannot be too far from earshot when James calls for such compassionate responses from its readers.

The moral exhortation in James, driven by so many imperatives, may come across as shrill to interpreters who take them as a disjointed collection of generic platitudes. Yet the source of all the letter's ethical energy, and the thing that gives cohesion to the multiple commands, is anything but a sense of dutiful moral rigor. The source is somewhat muted, but James attunes its audience's ears to recognize it: divine wisdom. Wisdom is God's gift for believers who have experienced a new "birth" and who participate in the fulfilling of God's "own purpose" (Jas 1:17–18). To ancient readers the letter's references to wisdom would have been familiar from Jewish sources and perhaps from philosophical traditions in the wider Greco-Roman context. For Jews wisdom referred to God's own self-expression in the world, something encountered not exclusively in temples or books but in the course of people's daily lives. Wisdom—which several Jewish texts depict as a personalized being, as a kind of embodiment of God and God's creative self-expression—was God's means of imprinting God's own self on all aspects of creation and human life. Wisdom is more than cleverness or moral intuition; it refers to God's ongoing presence and agency throughout the world. James is not alone in recognizing the Christian dimensions of wisdom; wisdom themes figure prominently also in John, 1 Corinthians, and Colossians.

For James, believers' access to divine wisdom is a core benefit of what other New Testament authors refer to as "the gospel." Wisdom is a key piece of James' theological perception of a God who remains active and accessible in the lives of God's people. James offers so much exhortation to its audience, not because the letter aspires primarily to build virtues or promote self-discipline, but because it wants believers to experience and promote the goodness and peace that God provides. Those divine gifts are available to Christ-followers even as they make their way through life as though they are a rootless, scattered people in an otherwise predatory and inimical human society that James refers to simply as "the world" (e.g., Jas 1:27; 4:4). As believers manifest divine wisdom in their deeds, they articulate who they are as dispersed tribes who have nevertheless become near to God (e.g., Jas 1:1, 4:8).

4

The First Letter of Peter

Confessing faith in Jesus Christ and being a member of a worshiping Christian community was not illegal in the first century, but in many settings identifying as a Christ-follower made a person appear unusual. As investigations of other New Testament books also reveal, when believers sought to live in ways that honored Christ and rejected other deities, there could be ramifications for how they circulated within the wider society and how that society treated them. Ancient people did not practice their religion as a purely personal or private affair; civic activities, public entertainment, business deals, education, and family gatherings all had unmistakable religious dimensions. Pronounced religious differences sometimes led to tension or even to backlash, and when that happened, Christ-followers found themselves confronted by questions: whether their Christian convictions were worth all of the trouble, whether they should respond to their social hardships—or even court them—in adversarial or subversive ways, and whether they should withdraw and totally disengage from their social contexts. If a Christian community was especially powerless or disheartened, that could affect how it perceived its options.

First Peter seeks to shape Christian self-understanding among believers who faced questions like those. The letter reinforces its audience's sense of themselves as outsiders who inhabit a world to which they do not fully belong. Yet those outsiders should not run away or brashly defy regnant values, according to 1 Peter. They should walk a delicate line that renounces old ways of living while embracing a self-disciplined morality that will give their opponents no cause to criticize their behavior. They should know that living as Christ-followers in their cultural context will invite criticism, yet they should not seek retribution or insist on their own rights. The core purpose of 1 Peter is relatively simple: the letter exhorts believers to aspire to moral self-control and to estimable behavior, which will help move their faith toward greater maturity as they await Christ's return and God's final judgment. Inspired by Christ's perseverance, believers should live in a conciliatory manner within a sociopolitical environment that directs scorn toward them.

The ways in which 1 Peter expresses its central purpose are more complicated, however. The letter's understanding of the specific shape of morality and faithful endurance speaks approvingly of suffering, almost as if incurring persecution is a sign of successful discipleship, a necessary aspect of faithful living. Perhaps the author saw no other option for his audience than to accept and celebrate unavoidable hardship in a uniquely hostile atmosphere. In any case, 1 Peter illustrates the challenges that first-century churches faced not just in enduring but also in making sense of their experiences. In addition, the book's more explicit theological reflections have been very influential in Christian theology and practice through the centuries, especially with regard to subjects such as the salvation accomplished by Jesus Christ, the church's relationship to the Roman Empire, and the proper behavior and standing of women and slaves.

The Letter's Origins and Ancient Audience

Exile and dislocation are primary themes in 1 Peter. The opening verse directs the letter to "the exiles of the Dispersion" in numerous Roman provinces throughout Asia Minor, which corresponds roughly to modern Turkey. Farther on in the letter, 1 Peter refers to its audience as "aliens and exiles" (1 Pet 2:11). The words do not necessarily mean that the document originally went out to Christ-followers who were migrants or displaced persons in a literal sense, either by their own choice or by official edict. Rather, the terminology evokes memories of the Jewish Scriptures, associating those believers with Abraham, as well as Israel and Judah, during times when God's people were separated from the land and autonomy that God had pledged to them. The language allows

1 Peter to tell its audience who they are, imparting a theological identity to them that integrates them into the overarching reach of God's history and purposes. As well as sojourners who await the full realization of God's promises to them, they collectively are also, according to 1 Peter, a new temple, a community of priests, a distinctive race, and a nation living apart from its true home.

Repeatedly the letter mentions the trials, sufferings, and adversity that its readers are facing or should expect to face. The outlook is general, without clearly indicating whether believers were in fact only targets of suspicion or whether they faced harsher treatment, such as prejudice, social and professional ostracism, legal censures, or outright violence. No evidence exists to indicate that Roman officials used violence to suppress Christian activity in Asia Minor during the first century, which therefore makes it very unlikely that 1 Peter has that particular kind of hardship in mind. Instead, probably the audience's embrace of Christian teachings had put them at odds with the dominant imperial culture and its civic expectations, or perhaps the letter writer merely wanted his audience to know that they should expect their beliefs and practices eventually to generate friction in their social, political, commercial, and even familial networks.

The audience members were entirely or mostly gentile, judging from several comments about their adoption of new practices and their inclusion into a new group (e.g., 1 Pet 1:3–4, 18; 2:9–10; 4:3–4). First Peter quotes frequently from the Septuagint and employs imagery from Jewish history, but that feature of the letter does not mean that its audience members had to have been Jewish. They very well could have been gentiles who were especially knowledgeable about the gospel's Jewish foundations. The more important point about the letter's interactions with Jewish traditions is that they assist the effort to socialize believers into a new theological identity. In other words, the letter renames its readers with scriptural terminology; they are not rootless wanderers, after all, but people claimed by God's own choosing and therefore participants in a long history filled with struggles and promises. Their theological identity separates them from the surrounding population, for 1 Peter refers to the Christ-followers in Asia Minor as people who live as aliens "among the Gentiles" (1 Pet 2:12), as if they have totally shed their former existence as gentiles or outcasts themselves, because God has claimed them (cf. 1 Thess 4:5).

Since the letter—like Ephesians, Colossians, 1 Timothy, and Titus—includes a household code, a list of instructions for various members of a household, it is reasonable to assume that 1 Peter was meant to influence family units. Various exhortations to the audience to maintain conventional household structures and to respect imperial authorities imply that some of those families were visible enough to have been at risk of losing honor or influence if their lifestyles deviated too far from cultural norms, or if the families were vulnerable enough to face perilous consequences for identifying themselves with Christ. The letter's specific commands to slaves indicate that some in the audience were owned by other people who might be especially abusive slave owners. Since 1 Peter includes no commands to slave masters, however, it appears that the letter imagines an audience—or audiences—composed primarily of less powerful and lower-class people. Frequent references to enduring harassment and slander suggest that the letter has in mind people who lacked the social capital that might have provided them recourse against the animosity their Christian identity triggered. In several respects, then, they were an at-risk people. Yet the letter insists they are supposed to be exactly that. Such is the life of exiles who await God's future, as 1 Peter understands the situation.

The Question of Authorship

Longstanding Christian traditions hold that one of Jesus' original disciples, Simon Peter, wrote this letter soon before his martyrdom around 64 CE. Those traditions locate Peter's death in Rome, which means at the very end of 1 Peter a reference to "Babylon" makes a derisive claim about the imperial capital. "Babylon" serves as a cipher for Rome repeatedly in Revelation, too.

Several features of the book cast serious doubt on the possibility that Peter wrote it, however. The syntax is relatively sophisticated and shows no real evidence that its author was influenced by knowledge of Aramaic or Hebrew, as Simon Peter surely was. It is also unlikely that a Galilean fisherman could have achieved such a level of Greek literary aptitude (cf. Acts 4:13). Assumptions throughout 1 Peter about social tensions besetting Christian groups in Asia Minor correspond better with evidence about conditions there near the end of the first century (such as Revelation, which also addresses itself to churches in Asia Minor) than they correspond with what can be reasonably hypothesized about churches' experiences there in the early 60s CE. The attempt to cast Rome as a new Babylon echoes other Jewish writings that did so to criticize Rome and to long for its downfall, especially after Roman forces ravaged Jerusalem at the end of the Great Revolt of 66–70.

There are no other writings to which one can compare 1 Peter to strengthen or weaken the proposal that it is a pseudepigraphic letter. Numerous other Christian writings from antiquity claim to have been written by Simon Peter, but all of them, including 2 Peter, were obviously written decades or more after his death. Because of Simon Peter's renown in Jesus' ministry and in the leadership of the early church (cf. Acts 1–12), he was a popular choice for many who wanted their writings to resonate with an apostle's authority and legacy.

When all the evidence is considered, the most plausible conclusion is that 1 Peter was composed after the destruction of the Jerusalem temple and written in Peter's name by an author seeking to bring Peter's prominence and his association with the church in Rome to bear on new circumstances, probably during the 70s or 80s. That conclusion need not be taken at face value. Although it comes from a much more intricate analysis of the letter than can be offered here, it still involves a degree of speculation.

All of the options for answers to the question of 1 Peter's authorship involve conjecture. Also, all of them have very minimal impact on how one might interpret what the letter says. The character, legacy, and spiritual authority of Simon Peter means almost nothing for the letter itself in terms of how the book presents its teachings or roots them in an author's distinctive knowledge or experiences. At the beginning the letter merely presents itself as the work of the apostle Peter. Near the end, it leans very briefly on Peter's authority as "an elder" and as one who witnessed Jesus' sufferings. When the letter's concluding section mentions Silvanus, probably as the person charged to deliver the document, and Mark, it does not clarify whether it is indicating the same Silvanus and Mark named elsewhere in the New Testament (e.g., Acts 12:25, 15:22; 2 Cor 1:19; Col 4:10; 1 Thess 1:1; 2 Thess 1:1; 2 Tim 4:11; Phlm 24). Both were common names in the Greco-Roman world. Brief references to them do not shine light into the letter's unknown origins. Interpreters nevertheless discover in 1 Peter a document that is interested more in instructing and shaping an audience than in reflecting on its own originating circumstances.

Overview

Salutation and Blessing (1 Pet 1:1–12)

After a brief salutation that emphasizes the addressees' identity as people chosen by "God the Father" and made holy by the Spirit, the letter offers a blessing to God (cf. 2 Cor 1:3–7, Eph 1:3–14). The salutation and blessing together introduce themes that will reappear later in 1 Peter, including the security of God's salvation, the need for ongoing obedience, and the reality of trials and tribulations that can reveal and refine people's faith.

The introductory sentences dwell on the certain yet currently incomplete nature of salvation. God has provided salvation as "a new birth into a living hope" through Jesus Christ's resurrection. Believers possess an unfailing inheritance from the God who protects them, even though they still wait for "a salvation ready to be revealed in the last time," the time of Jesus Christ's revelation (*apokalupsis*). Jesus remains unseen now, yet this does not prevent his followers from loving him, believing in him, and growing into the fullness of their salvation.

To bolster certitude about that salvation, the author offers the first of several short theological explanations that appear in the letter. In this case, 1 Peter claims that "the Spirit of Christ" formerly guided Israel's and Judah's prophets, causing their oracles to speak in advance about Christ's sufferings and glory (1 Pet 1:11). The explanation tells the letter's audience that they express beliefs and hopes that are by no means new things; even gentile believers occupy a place in the long lineage of Jewish expectation and confidence. Moreover, the salvation of gentiles does not represent a new or unforeseen development in God's plans. While God's ultimate intentions have yet to be fully realized, they have nevertheless been disclosed previously throughout the history and struggles of God's people. By showing the audience their connections to a larger community of God's people, 1 Peter seeks to impart strength and cohesion to them so they can endure the trials they face.

Disciplined Obedience and New Identity (1 Pet 1:13–2:10)

In this interim time, as believers await their inheritance, the full revealing of their salvation, they should pursue a holy way of life. The challenge of doing so requires disciplined determination in addition to hope, for believers need to resist the desires that compelled them when they previously lived in ignorance of God's blessings. Another explanatory aside provides the theological basis for the letter's perspective on Christian conduct: the ransom paid to free believers from "the futile ways inherited from [their] ancestors" was Christ's own blood, an utterly reliable and precious currency (1 Pet 1:18–19). Believers therefore can understand themselves as part of God's eternal intentions, as claimed through the decisive and transformative power of "the living and enduring word of God" (1 Pet 1:23). Knowing these transcendent realities inspires "reverent fear" that motivates obedience among those who expect to benefit from the revelation of God's purposes through Jesus Christ.

The letter commands readers to shed common vices, but the process by which believers will "grow into salvation" (1 Pet 2:2) involves more than personal moral exertion. God is responsible, for God constructs people's lives into something new. God builds people into a new temple and a priesthood, for God has laid Christ as a cornerstone for a new organic structure, as the author interprets various texts from the Septuagint (Isa 28:16, Ps 118:22, Isa 8:14). God's agency creates a new identity for believers, making them into "a chosen race, a royal priesthood, a holy nation, God's own people." Those names and images in 1 Pet 2:9 come from scriptural texts (e.g., Exod 19:5–6; Deut 7:6; Isa 43:20–21; Hos 2:23; cf. Rev 1:6), and they reassert the audience's identity as a privileged and select people who enjoy access to God and security from God. When 1 Peter calls for obedience, therefore, it frames believers' conduct and cooperation as congruous with their new identity.

Honorable Conduct and Orderly Households (1 Pet 2:11–3:12)

This section begins with another warning about the need to assert control over "desires" (cf. 1 Pet 1:14; 4:2–3), yet in this case the motives for doing so include earning honor from those outside of the community of faith (curiously, 1 Peter, like all of the General Letters except for James and 3 John, never uses the word *church*). The importance of making a positive impression on outsiders explains the need for believers to submit themselves to civil authorities, since living in conformity with imperial leaders and expectations will neutralize the ignorant criticisms of opponents. In what may be one of the most accommodationist passages in the New Testament, 1 Peter intimates that even the Roman emperor deserves honor (1 Pet 2:13–17; cf. Rom 13:1–7).

The accent on conforming to conventional imperial expectations continues in a series of commands to slaves, wives, and husbands. Like the household codes elsewhere in the New Testament (Eph 5:21–6:9, Col 3:18–4:1; cf. 1 Tim 6:1–2, Titus 2:1–10), this one commends lifestyles in which various members of a social hierarchy perform their appointed roles, based on common understandings of how Roman society functioned according to the relative value of husbands, wives, and slaves.

At the same time, several aspects of 1 Peter's household code distinguish it from the others in the New Testament. It addresses a smaller number of household members. The instructions to slaves are rather stringent, if not cruel. Harsh masters deserve a slave's submission as much as kind ones do, according to 1 Peter. Moreover, those slaves who suffer violence even when they "do right" receive divine approval. The letter's effort to incentivize a slave's obedience to an abusive master in this way may have been driven by an intent to make the Christian community appear nonsubversive in the Roman world, but of course there have been disastrous moral consequences throughout history when that ethic has led Christians to excuse brutality by slave owners—to say nothing of excusing slavery in general—or to valorize dehumanizing forms of victimization, as if somehow those who suffer enjoy additional and unique opportunities to please God.

First Peter does not dwell on the particular kinds of suffering that ancient slaves received from their masters. Instead, the letter offers another theological aside to hold up Christ's sufferings as an example for slaves to imitate. The tangential explanation in 1 Pet 2:21–25 refers to Isa 53:9 and describes Jesus as an acquiescent victim, thereby giving insight into how some currents in early Christian thought interpreted Jesus' passion against the backdrop of Isa 53:5–11. Yet interpreters can also note that in this aside 1 Peter offers a clumsy and potentially dangerous comparison between Christ's passion and the sufferings of slaves. Most slaves of violent masters had no option but to endure physical, sexual, and emotional abuse, while Christ chose his fate willingly, as 1 Peter implies. It is one thing for someone, like Jesus, to choose to endure one's own unavoidable suffering for the sake of a greater purpose. It is a very different thing for someone else, like the letter's author, to encourage or compel other people to suffer violence, particularly if it is a manner of violence that the encourager does not have to fear for himself. Anyone who casually refers to this section of 1 Peter as a means of exhorting those who face any kinds of physical and emotional suffering, especially suffering that stems from abuse, to endure their pain without complaint has failed to account for the problematic nature of the letter's comparison between slaves and Christ, and has neglected the ways in which other biblical passages offer competing perspectives on faithful living and advocating on behalf of those who are powerless.

Commands to wives and husbands assume the superiority of husbands, as one would expect from a first-century document. The letter tells wives that submission to an unbelieving husband may lead him to express faith in Christ. Coming directly on the heels of the unyielding instructions to slaves, the commands to wives appear to imply that there are no limits to what a wife should endure in her quest to be subservient to a spouse. Indeed, one especially appalling legacy of these verses' interpretation has been the galling practice of telling victims of domestic violence that they might see their partners transformed if only they patiently endure mistreatment and put aside their fears for their own security.

The instructions that 1 Peter offers to men are very short by comparison. They call husbands to "show consideration" and give "honor" to wives. Implied in the commands are the need to show patience and forbearance with a man's existential inferior, since the letter refers to women as "the weaker sex," or literally, "the weaker vessel" (1 Pet 3:7). While this characterization justifiably shocks many modern readers, it aligns the book with a rather commonplace ancient understanding—common among men, at least—that women were physiologically, emotionally, and intellectually deficient in comparison to men.

A concluding appeal for unity and love addresses everyone in the letter's audience. By quoting the Septuagint version of Ps 34:12–16 in 1 Pet 3:10–12, the appeal associates God's favor with those who pursue peace and resist the urge to retaliate against the people who harm them. Given how the rest of the letter refers to the audience as suffering some kind of strife, it appears that the instructions in this section commend a strategy of de-escalation. First Peter tells believers who may feel vulnerable that they should do all they can to model respectable behavior. Given what the ancient social mores were, the letter's notion of respectability may have been easier and less costly for the free men in the letter's audience than it was for their wives and the slaves in their community.

Enduring Suffering and Conforming to God's Will (1 Pet 3:13–4:19)

The prospect of hardship remains front and center in this section, which places so much value on doing "what is right" (1 Pet 3:14, translating the Greek word usually rendered elsewhere in the New Testament as "righteousness" or "justification"; cf. 1 Pet 2:24) that it considers suffering to be a worthwhile side effect. The letter does not say much about how exactly to define "what is right," however. The previous section praised conventional social hierarchies and a willingness to endure abuse. This one speaks in general terms about resolutely confessing "Christ as Lord" (1 Pet 3:15).

Instead of extolling specific kinds of behavior, the letter embarks on another theological aside in 1 Pet 3:18–22 to explain the extent of Christ the Lord's authority and the range of the salvation he accomplished. Christ visited and preached to "the spirits in prison," an ambiguous phrase that probably refers to a netherworld where the crucified Jesus encountered the souls of the people God destroyed in the great flood described in Genesis 6–8. Christian tradition has expanded the scope of this part of 1 Peter and used it to support a more comprehensive belief that Christ went to hell between the crucifixion and the resurrection in order to liberate everyone there from Satan's power (cf. 1 Pet 4:6). Whatever the precise meaning of 1 Peter's referent, the theological aside goes on to say that, following the resurrection, Christ went to heaven, where he enjoys all of God's authority over all "angels, authorities, and powers." The overall point of the theological explanation is much simpler than an attempt to delineate a doctrine about salvation and Christ's specific whereabouts between Good Friday and Easter Sunday. First Peter implores its audience to know that if Christ has such all-encompassing authority over the whole cosmos, and if Christ saves believers just as surely as God preserved Noah and his family, then the struggles that Jesus' followers face now look less threatening by comparison and certainly far from ultimate. No believer—perhaps no one else, either—resides beyond Christ's reach.

Even with all of the authority and majesty that was his, Christ also "suffered in the flesh" (1 Pet 4:1). The trials believers face are therefore not aberrations; they are manifestations of God's will, and believers should embrace them as opportunities to share in Christ's own sufferings. Indignities suffered are, according to 1 Peter, a mark of honor because they associate believers with Christ—the same Christ who serves as the ground of believers' confidence in God's fidelity. This confidence buoys Christ-followers as they await the divine judgment that stands near at hand.

Concluding Exhortations, Greetings, and Benediction (1 Pet 5)

As 1 Peter draws to a close, it offers instructions addressed specifically to the leaders of Christian communities, the "elders" who "tend the flock of God" (1 Pet 5:1–2; cf. Acts 14:23, 1 Tim 5:17, Titus 1:5, Jas 5:14). Just as previously in the letter Christ served as a model to imitate for people who suffer, likewise the communities' elders should strive to be examples to those under their authority. Final exhortations highlight the importance of humility and, again, self-discipline. Images of both danger and reassurance provide the last pieces of motivation: the devil lurks as an active threat, and God will finally "restore, support, strengthen, and establish" (1 Pet 5:10) the letter's audience of dispersed, harassed, bedeviled, and waiting believers.

The Letter's Themes and Theological Emphases

Trials and Suffering

Many passages in 1 Peter assume the audience is experiencing some kind of persecution as a backlash against their Christian faith and conduct (e.g., 1 Pet 1:6; 3:9, 13–17; 4:4, 12–19; 5:9–10). A key assumption propels the letter: Christian communities, at least those in the author's and audience's contexts, will always be suffering communities. The wounds Christ-followers will suffer will not necessarily be bloody or life-threatening, but things like social ostracism, economic boycotts, and a deep sense of alienation can have their own destructive effects on people. The letter's assumptions have sometimes led Christians in many eras and settings to conclude that authentic faith must always generate animosity or ridicule from outsiders. That point of view can lend courage and hope to churches that truly suffer from genuine persecution, although it can also create downright pathological attitudes among Christians in tolerant societies who nevertheless seek opportunities to insist they are being victimized.

The letter's frequent appeals to hardship, combined with its consistent effort to incorporate its audience into a collective identity as a people who belong to God and have connections to ancient Israel, likely reassured ancient readers that the trials they faced were nothing unusual and that their struggles could be endured. First Peter strengthens its audience's resolve by building their sense of solidarity (e.g., 1 Pet 2:9–10; 5:9). Christ's own example as one who suffered also provides motivation (e.g., 1 Pet 2:21–24; 3:18; 4:1–2, 13). In the end, however, the solutions the letter advances probably illustrate the relative powerlessness that characterized most Christian communities in the Roman Empire at that time. With no political leverage, all they could finally control was their own moral choices, which may explain why 1 Peter puts such a premium on "good conduct" (e.g., 1 Pet 3:16). Perhaps those communities' odds for survival appeared so tenuous that the author believed they had few options but to deflect the dominant society's suspicions away from them by behaving well. Conforming to conventional household structures and hierarchies and giving honor to the emperor might mitigate the persecution, for showing respect to the emperor and to the Roman cultural ethos might fulfill civic obligations in a minimalistic yet still visible way.

First Peter comes close to glorifying suffering when it associates suffering with being blessed and rejoicing (1 Pet 3:14; 4:12–14; cf. Jas 1:2). A warm embrace of suffering betrays itself as acutely problematic when the letter commends slaves who suffer violence from their owners (1 Pet 2:20–21). When the book suggests that suffering is sometimes "God's will" (1 Pet 3:17, 4:19; cf. 1:11), it raises questions about what exactly God's intentions might be and whether the patient endurance of suffering must be an unqualified Christian virtue. First Peter does not pause to offer nuanced explanations or to answer those who would reject the suggestion that suffering can serve positive purposes; the book's attention looks in other directions.

The questions 1 Peter provokes about suffering and endurance, or about abuse and victimization, are never easy and should prompt interpreters to bring other biblical books into creative and corrective conversation with 1 Peter. It is also crucial for interpreters to keep in mind that 1 Peter appears to have one particular type of suffering in mind: negative consequences that people experience because of their efforts to live out their faith and to resist evil. The letter never celebrates gratuitous suffering, such as what comes from chronic pain, disease, natural disasters, military action, hunger, and heartbreak. It understands the world to be a dangerous place, a terrain populated by the forces described in Jewish apocalyptic writings: the devil and other spiritual beings—"authorities" and "powers" (1 Pet 5:8, 3:22)—that oppose God and the people of God. The cosmic landscape makes it inevitable, 1 Peter says, that particular forms of resistance will lash out against those who "do good" (1 Pet 4:19). Until the revealing (*apokalupsis*) of Jesus Christ and his glory comes to pass (1 Pet 1:5, 7, 12, 13; 4:13; 5:1), believers inhabit a threatening environment as aliens who do not really belong. The trials they endure as a consequence of their virtuous behavior may be damaging, but at least those hardships cannot separate Christ-followers from "the guardian of [their] souls" (1 Pet 2:25).

The history of 1 Peter's interpretation issues a stark reminder that the book's teachings on trials, suffering, and patience need to be handled with care. The basic reasoning and cultural outlook that undergird 1 Peter's exhortations and reassurances have had different effects on different kinds of audiences. If one reads the letter as a broken and harassed author encouraging other broken people who are near the point of collapsing under the weight of hopelessness, that is one thing. If the letter is taken to be the words of a comfortable church leader trying to pacify powerless people in a distant land by making them content with their sorry lot in life, that is an egregious thing. How 1 Peter might have helped or damaged an ancient audience remains impossible to reconstruct with certainty. How the letter might help or damage new audiences depends on how modern interpreters adopt or criticize the letter's perspectives concerning suffering and its ostensible benefits.

Jesus Christ's Role in Salvation

With so much of the letter's focus fixed on the task of equipping its audience to be resolute and self-disciplined, 1 Peter does not put its primary efforts into teaching Christ-followers about a range of theological themes. Yet this observation hardly means to suggest that the book does not provide theological insights. When the letter periodically provides a theological explanation to support a specific exhortation, especially an exhortation about resisting the impulse to retaliate against one's persecutors, it allows interpreters to observe ways in which people in ancient churches understood Jesus Christ's role in God's commitment to provide salvation. First Peter offers little more than hints from which to derive insights into those understandings, for the letter keeps its theological explanations short, perhaps because the author assumed his audience was already familiar with his ideas.

The verses that mention Jesus preaching to "the spirits in prison" (1 Pet 3:19) and "the dead" (1 Pet 4:6) have been noted already as inspirations for the Christian confession that the crucified Jesus "descended into hell" prior to his resurrection. Whether or not those brief and enigmatic parts of the letter really support the more expansive and detailed doctrines that would eventually arise from them, clearly 1 Peter says at least that death cannot finally obstruct the effects and reach of God's salvation (cf. Rom 5:18). Because of where Jesus has gone, there is no place where the message of salvation has not been declared or cannot be heard.

Additional theological explanations in the letter are noteworthy due to the influence they have had in Christian theology. Drawing from the Septuagint version of Isa 53:5–11 and its description of an anonymous innocent sufferer, 1 Pet 2:21–25 considers Jesus sinless and one who "bore our sins in his body on the cross." The letter also refers to salvation as a ransom, or a liberating exchange, associated with Jesus' blood, for 1 Peter likens Jesus to "a lamb without defect or blemish" (1 Pet 1:18–19), which recalls the requirements for a Passover lamb in Exod 12:5 and for sacrifices in Lev 22:21. With those sundry claims, the broader rhetorical point the book makes about Jesus is that his acceptance of undeserved suffering provides an example for his followers, yet some of those claims have also prompted the Christian church throughout history to generate deeper reflections on the nature of salvation. In particular, those passages have made 1 Peter an influential book in conversations about atonement, the question of how salvation occurs through Jesus' death.

The letter's references to blood, suffering, and innocence have fueled proposals about Jesus functioning as a sacrifice for sin. Such proposals claim, to oversimplify the matter, that at the heart of Christian salvation is a sacrificed Savior who must suffer the penalty of sin, even though this victim himself does not deserve such misery (cf. 1 Cor 5:7; Heb 9:11–14, 26). Jesus' death, according to those proposals, is a vicarious act, in which he substitutes himself as a victim in the place of a humanity who truly deserved the punishment. Among all the perspectives on Jesus' death presented in the New Testament, that one is far from dominant, although it has come to manifest itself frequently in churches' hymns, liturgical symbols, and popular articulations of Christian beliefs. It is a perspective on atonement that remains theologically controversial among many modern Christians, given what it typically presumes about God requiring a transaction to occur before God can grant forgiveness, about Jesus becoming a victim through divine coercion, and about raw suffering as the means of discovering redemptive power and renewal.

Underlying the numerous theological statements in 1 Peter is a foundational conviction that God is engaged with the world and has been throughout history. The book's frequent references to a future time when salvation and glory will be "revealed" indicate that God will yet bring all things to their expected conclusion. That conclusion is already under way, given that Jesus has received authority over all angelic and cosmic powers (1 Pet 3:22; cf. Acts 2:32–36, Eph 1:20–23, Rev 5:11–13). God's people can firmly expect to participate in the ultimate glory to come, even if their current state of existence looks far less glorious, leaving them feeling outnumbered and vulnerable. Jesus emerges from the letter as a model for downtrodden believers to imitate not in light of the power he has come to possess but because of his willingness to endure hardship in his passion. He did not pursue retribution against those who demeaned him, like any honorable Roman man would have been expected to do. Rather, Jesus expected his compliance would lead to the salvation of others. First Peter leads a possibly antagonized audience to expect the same, even though they themselves are not Jesus (e.g., 1 Pet 2:12; 3:1–2, 15–16).

Jewish Scriptures and Believers' Identity

With so many quotations of scriptural texts and allusions to others, 1 Peter illustrates a point commonly seen in additional New Testament writings: the earliest generations of Christ-followers made sense of who they were, who God is, and what Christ had done by drawing from Jewish Scriptures. The letter relies on Scripture to make sense of its audience's identity as sojourners who are awaiting the time when God's pledges will become realities. Scripture serves to establish the basic continuity between God's previous work and the "new birth" that occurs through Jesus' resurrection.

First Peter offers an example of how early Christ-followers read the Jewish Scriptures. They did so from a christological vantage point, meaning that they considered those writings in light of Jesus Christ and what they had come to believe about him. For example, 1 Pet 1:10–12 asserts that prophets of Israel and Judah were guided by "the Spirit of Christ" and that they originally divulged details about the salvation that would come through Christ. Understanding the Old Testament prophets like that can threaten to ignore the ways in which the prophets spoke God's word to their own contemporary settings. Even scriptural passages that the New Testament explicitly cites to interpret Christ and his work were not necessarily originally meant as predictions of the gospel. For example, nothing in existing literature indicates that Jews prior to the time of Jesus interpreted the so-called Servant Songs in Isaiah (e.g., Isa 52:13–53:12) as speaking about a specific future deliverer. However, the author of 1 Peter looks back on that material and sees in it a prefiguration of Christ's death (1 Pet 2:22; cf. Acts 8:32–33). This attempt by the letter's author to read Jesus into certain Old Testament passages attempts to express a unity of God's activity throughout history; its primary point is to insist that Jesus be understood as representing not a totally new direction in God's intentions but the fulfillment of them.

Despite the nuances of the book's appeals to scriptural texts, Christian interpreters have sometimes taken 1 Peter and other New Testament writings (e.g., Matt 1:22–23; Luke 24:44-47; John 5:46; Gal 3:8; 1 Cor 15:3–4; Heb 7:1–10) as a license for denying that ancient Jewish texts can mean anything else of consequence other than to describe or predict Jesus. As discussed with reference to Hebrews, it is sometimes a short step from those kinds of interpretive assumptions to a denial of Judaism's own theological validity. First Peter does not provide enough detail to reveal what exactly its author thought about Judaism and its enduring value. It could be that 1 Peter aims to incorporate gentile Christ-followers, as themselves a "chosen" people (1 Pet 1:2), into the wider and older family of God that began with God's promises to Abraham. It could be that 1 Peter understands the Jewish Scriptures as having a plurality of possible meanings as testimonies to the salvation God repeatedly accomplishes on behalf of God's people. Yet history teems with reminders of the deadly and destructive consequences that follow when Christians take hasty or dubious interpretations of 1 Peter and other ancient Christian writings as grounds for a supersessionist understanding of Christianity. Because of the grave outcomes that come from those kinds of perspectives, interpretation of 1 Peter—or, for that matter, any biblical text—never ceases to be serious business.

5

The Second Letter of Peter

Second Peter dedicates itself to equipping Christ-followers to survive and endure, and especially to navigate their way when confronted with various options for living their faith. The book urges its audience to trust the traditions associated with the apostles and to reject new teachings. It counsels ongoing patience concerning Christ's return. It refuses to surrender confident hope that the ultimate fulfillment of God's promises, including the establishment of "new heavens and a new earth" (2 Pet 3:13; cf. Isa 65:17, 66:22; Rev 21:1), is on its way. The relatively short document does not lay out a comprehensive theological vision but vigorously tries to persuade an audience to hold fast to the teachings they already know. Second Peter makes its case with determined theological assertions, an unwavering embrace of established traditions, earnest exhortations to remain resolute in one's faith, irate condemnation of opponents, and fearsome threats about God's coming judgment. With pronounced rhetorical seriousness, it declares the stakes are high.

The kinds of concerns the letter expresses, along with its confident and almost authoritarian tone, suggest that 2 Peter speaks to a time and place in which uncertainty held sway among one or more groups of Christ-followers. It addresses people who may have been rattled by the fact that Jesus had not yet returned. It speaks about the church's apostles as though they were no longer present. On the whole, it assumes its audience found themselves facing challenges brought on by transitions.

For those and other reasons, 2 Peter apparently belongs to a period in the early churches' journeys when teachings and memories associated with the original apostles were still in circulation but so too were alternate ways of articulating Christian beliefs. In such a setting, disagreement about what it meant to believe and live in an authentically Christian manner was bound to percolate. In that kind of a climate, 2 Peter rejects those who would abandon traditional beliefs and sharply cautions those who might grow lax in pursuing a virtuous life as a means of strengthening their faithfulness.

The Letter's Origins and Ancient Audience

Because 2 Peter does not refer to specific places or specific people among its audience, it is impossible to offer precise proposals about who its original recipients were and what circumstances they inhabited. The book addresses itself in its first verse merely to "those who have received a faith as precious as ours," making it sound less like an occasional letter composed for specific purposes and more like an instructional treatise or a sermon intended for broad distribution. Distinctive imagery and themes in the document owe themselves to the influence of Hellenistic thought, which could mean that the letter's author and original audience were acquainted with discussing Christian principles with a peculiarly Hellenistic, particularly Stoic, accent.

Although the document expresses an expectation that Simon Peter, its attributed author, will die soon (2 Pet 1:13–15), that statement hardly rules out the possibility—actually, a very strong probability—that someone else wrote the letter after the apostle Peter died, which happened around 64 CE. The book speaks of people who mock Christian hopes about Christ's return because that event still had not occurred. The patient outlook that 2 Peter adopts toward the prospect of Jesus' *parousia*, his next "coming," offers one hint that the document comes from a later point in time, perhaps even decades after Peter's death and the destruction of the Jerusalem temple in 70 CE. Additionally, the author speaks of Paul's letters, reports that some people find those writings difficult to understand, and warns against teachers who dangerously twist the letters' true meaning. Second Peter explicitly groups Paul's letters with other pieces of "Scripture"—not necessarily a formal designation in the first and second centuries, yet one indicating that Paul's letters had accumulated very significant renown and authority in some

Christian communities. It would have taken time for Paul's letters to circulate and attract that kind of widespread attention and respect after he wrote them in the 50s CE, further suggesting a later date for 2 Peter.

While the letter offers many pieces of evidence that inform lasting debates about who wrote 2 Peter and when it was written, those aspects of the book also indicate that its audience, whoever they were, found themselves living in a time in which people were questioning what made for reliable sources of their religious and theological knowledge. To reinforce its audience's faithful resolve, the letter reasserts the importance of the Jewish Scriptures, the testimony of the apostles, and the teachings of Paul. It also sternly cautions against "false teachers" who would corrupt and show contempt for trustworthy traditions. In short, 2 Peter expresses deep concern about Christian communities that appear to be drifting further and further from their original ways of expressing the Christian message and living the Christian life. As a result, the letter endeavors to rebuild the connections.

The Question of Authorship

Even though the letter attributes itself to Simon Peter, a significant amount of evidence from the book itself casts doubt on that claim. Observations of the evidence are not purely a modern pursuit; even some Christian authors who wrote in the second, third, and fourth centuries refused to grant that the apostle Peter could have actually written 2 Peter. Second Peter's own use of source material, themes, and style seems to indicate the letter originally addressed itself to circumstances in the early churches' experiences that materialized well after Peter's death. Regarding the book's use of source material, parts of the letter exhibit great similarity to content from Jude. Analysis of the correspondences between the two writings indicates that the author of 2 Peter used Jude as a source. The book's reliance on Jude obviously means that Jude was written first, but the challenges of assigning a date to Jude with confidence make it difficult to use that book to locate 2 Peter's origins with any greater precision. The themes of 2 Peter reveal more, however. Particular characteristics—especially the letter's attempts to assuage anxieties about Christ's extended absence, the high regard given to Paul's writings, and the Stoic flavor of selected imagery and appeals—indicate that the book probably did not originate during the first or second generation of the Christian church. Finally, the distinctive style of

2 Peter casts further doubt on the possibility that the letter came about during Peter's lifetime, or even in the first century, for that matter. Much of the book's distinctive vocabulary was more common in the early second century than it was in the mid-first century. The detailed arguments behind proposals to locate 2 Peter in the early second century turn out to be quite persuasive. If indeed it came into being between 110 and 120 CE, then it was likely the last of all the New Testament documents to be written.

To suggest that 2 Peter originated after Peter's death as a pseudepigraphic writing and probably during the early decades of the second century should not imply a negative judgment on what the book says. The effort of inquiring about the letter's author and date means to assist in making sense of where the book stands in the history of the early church and to understand how the letter's distinctive message aimed to help an audience that was apparently experiencing a transition into a new era. It also bears noting that the hypothesis that Simon Peter did not write the document does not answer the question of who did instead. No one knows who wrote 2 Peter. The authors of 1 Peter and Jude almost certainly did not, for 2 Peter's style differs substantially from those two books.

Furthermore, no one can say exactly why an ancient author might have chosen to attribute this specific letter to Simon Peter as opposed to another leader from the first generation of the Christian church. The apostle Peter's onetime prominence among Jewish Christ-followers and law-observant Christian communities (e.g., Acts 11:1–18, 15:1–21; Gal 1:18–2:10) may have made his legacy especially influential among those groups, which were shrinking in size and vitality in the early second century. Peter's traditional associations with the church in Rome may also have helped the letter speak on behalf of the Christian movement in Rome or on behalf of Christ-followers who were especially sympathetic to the church there. Memories of historical tensions between Peter and Paul (e.g., Gal 2:11–14) may have encouraged the creation of a document like this one, a book written in Peter's name that esteems Paul's letters. The irenic display of appreciation could be an attempt to heal wounded relationships between the respective admirers of those two widely influential apostles. Subtly depicting Peter and Paul as a united team would have bolstered people's confidence in established apostolic traditions during a time when some leaders were growing increasingly worried about the possibility of believers departing from the church's traditional foundations.

Whoever the author and whatever the motive behind the letter's associations with Simon Peter, still the book evokes those associations only very gently, referring to Peter just a few times and not explicitly capitalizing on his particular teachings, his experiences as one of Jesus' original disciples (except for a reference to Peter's presence at Jesus' transfiguration), or his reputation as a faithful and effective leader in the early church. Assuming 2 Peter is a pseudepigraphic writing, one can view it as an attempt to lend the gravity of the apostle's voice and stature to certain Christian communities' efforts to contend against novel or contrary teachings. Yet by and large the letter expresses its theological perspective and makes its own argument without excessive reliance on Peter's specific legacy. In the end, then, the question of who wrote the book might fade in importance in comparison to the questions of what it says and how it goes about trying to shape an audience.

Overview

Because of the similarities between 2 Peter and Jude, people often study the two books together as a pair, allowing for ease of comparison and contrast. Because of the relatively obvious indications that the author of 2 Peter incorporated parts of Jude into his letter, meaning that Jude was composed previously to 2 Peter, readers may benefit from examining Jude first or in tandem with 2 Peter. Both the current chapter and chapter 7 in this volume treat material and themes that apply to both writings.

Salutation and Theological Summary (2 Pet 1:1–15)

Although the salutation of 2 Peter looks like the salutations of other letters in the New Testament, the nonspecific pastoral exhortations in 2 Peter make the book appear more like a theological tract than a particular piece of correspondence crafted for a specific community. Nevertheless, the salutation claims Simon Peter as the document's author, referring to him with the Aramaic form of his given name, Simeon (cf. Acts 15:14). The salutation also highlights the value of "knowledge," a fitting detail for a document that will go on to emphasize the importance of correct beliefs.

Instead of offering an opening thanksgiving or prayer, the letter extols God's gift of "everything needed for life and godliness." This gift involves "promises" that will lead to people becoming "participants of the divine nature" (2 Pet 1:3–4). The letter does not define this "divine nature" with precision, even though the expression was familiar—and variously employed—in multiple streams of Hellenistic philosophy and religion. Given the term's usage in other literature and the emphases of the wider context in 2 Peter, "divine nature" likely refers to immortality and holiness.

Immediately after speaking about what God provides, the letter flips the coin to describe what the audience must do as a consequence of God's generosity: 2 Peter calls them to "support [their] faith" with virtuous behavior and endurance. Those specific encouragements resonate with similar moral advice offered by ancient Stoic philosophers. Emphasis on virtue, endurance, and memory leads into the author's statement of the document's purpose. Second Peter means to reinforce people's knowledge of their obligations to God while also encouraging them that they are already "established in the truth that has come to [them]" (2 Pet 1:12). Believers' task, then, is to commit themselves to faithful perseverance, which involves resisting false teachings that deviate from established theological and ethical norms. The letter frames its exhortations as a gift and commission from an apostle himself, for 2 Peter expresses its message as one of Peter's last pastoral acts before he dies. Harnessing the pathos inherent in a revered teacher's desire to instruct his followers one last time before dying, 2 Peter adopts the persuasive rhetoric of Jewish testamentary literature, a type of writing imitated also in 2 Timothy.

Reliable and False Teachings (2 Pet 1:16–2:22)

Teachings associated with Peter and the other apostles possess a unique reliability, 2 Peter contends, because of those people's original connections to Jesus. In particular, the apostles' teachings about Jesus' future return in glory are not fabricated "myths," for they derive from the apostles' unique encounters with both Jesus' and his divine Father's "majesty." A specific example of the apostles' experience of that majesty occurred when Peter and others saw Jesus transfigured and heard God speak from the heavens (e.g., Mark 9:2–8 and parallels). The apostles—as well as the teachings they passed along to others—therefore can perceive the validity of certain unspecified prophecies, derived from the Jewish Scriptures, that ensure Christ will return. In contrast to false teachers, who distort those Scriptures, the ancient prophets and Jesus' apostles alike enjoyed a privileged access to God's own insights, and so they can be trusted when they asserted the certainty of Christ's eventual return, which will be the occasion for God to show the full reality of God's power. Even if the Lord's "coming" (*parousia*) has yet to occur, the apostles and their instructions remain trustworthy guides in the meantime.

In contrast to those reliable prophets and apostles, "false prophets" have always been a problem. Likewise, "false teachers" create persistent challenges for the letter's audience. The discussion of those people in 2 Pet 2:1–18 incorporates and expands material from Jude 4–13. Similarly to Jude, 2 Peter refrains from summarizing specific rival teachings that the author wishes to discredit. Both books prefer, instead, to characterize people associated with other teachings as stealthy and exploitative outsiders who live immoral lives. It does not necessarily follow from those characterizations that 2 Peter takes aim at antinomian movements within the Christian church, embodied in people who believed that the law of Moses and moral obligations were rendered obsolete because of the magnitude of God's grace. Neither is it clear that those teachers represented churches that had been heavily influenced by gnostic or Epicurean thought, as some interpreters propose. Accusations about insincere or predatory motives and immoral behavior were common tools for ancient authors to repudiate their ideological adversaries, and so it remains quite possible that 2 Peter is more interested in issuing a general condemnation than it is in describing or debating specific behaviors and teachings. This could have made the letter widely applicable in a number of settings and among relatively diverse audiences.

Like Jude does, 2 Peter consistently issues a dire assurance to discredit the teachings and people that reputedly threaten authentic Christian faith: God will not refrain from punishing those who are rebellious and disobedient. Repeatedly the letter insists that spiritual consequences follow from how one lives. References to sinful angels (Gen 6:1–4; cf. 1 Enoch 6–19), the deliverance of Noah's family through the flood (Gen 6:5–9:19), Sodom and Gomorrah (Gen 18:16–19:29), and Balaam (Num 22:1–40) all claim that God will punish those who resist God and defy God's moral expectations (2 Pet 2:4–16). Some of the references also contain a reassurance to faithful people, reminding them that God "knows how to rescue the godly," such as Noah and Lot, even when they find themselves surrounded by immorality.

The thick contempt for those called "false teachers" holds out no hope for their redemption (cf. Jude 22–23), although in the final chapter the letter will speak generally of God's desire for "all to come to repentance" (2 Pet 3:9). Second Peter emphasizes the tragedy of the rival teachers' condition: they are no garden-variety villains but people who identify as Christ-followers and could have been considered insiders at one point in time. "They have left the straight road and gone astray," for they once knew "the way of righteousness" and veered off of it (2 Pet 2:15, 21). They returned to the sinful deeds they formerly practiced, like a dog that cannot stop being enticed by its own vomit (Prov 26:11) and a washed pig that instinctually returns to the mud. This form of condemning rival teachers imputes a sense of tragedy to the situation, for the letter asserts that they have willfully rejected what they once knew to be true. They are not ignorant of the truth as much as they have consciously spurned it.

The brand of rhetoric 2 Peter directs toward opponents grew increasingly popular among Christian authors later in the second century and beyond. Some church leaders at that time employed a comparable strategy of vilifying their theological opposition when they engaged in fierce verbal battles against various sects within the church, which they labeled "heresies" (a word derived from a Greek term meaning "choices," which also appears as "opinions" in the NRSV rendering of 2 Pet 2:1). Characterizing one's ideological enemies as people who *choose* to be enemies to the truth they once knew and embraced makes them come across as much more sinister than enemies who are stupid outsiders or natural-born hucksters. Accusing people of having turned their back on God also allows authors to tell a cautionary tale, for such a story warns an audience that danger lurks at the door when believers neglect to cultivate their knowledge of God and the gifts that God provides through Christ. The author of 2 Peter does not want the letter's audience to presume that they can live passive, carefree lives. Insiders can go back to being outsiders if they do not remain resolute and vigilant.

Waiting for the Day of the Lord Faithfully (2 Pet 3)

The final chapter begins with reiteration. It refers in passing to a previous letter also written in Peter's name, and it exhorts the audience to remember what the prophets and apostles said, for they remain the basis of reliable and authoritative teachings. In addition, once again the author cautions that others will arise to oppose the church's foundational teachings.

A specific focus of the conflicts between the reliable traditions and the challenges brought by other people is the expectation of Christ's *parousia*. Self-indulgent "scoffers" can easily mock this expectation because the event has not yet occurred. In response, 2 Peter argues first that creation has never been a continually perpetuating system in which things always "continue as they were from the beginning" (2 Pet 3:4). Rather, the world once experienced God's disruptive and widely destructive judgment in the form of water—a flood. Likewise, judgment and devastation will derange everything again, the next time with fire. The only book in the New Testament to do so, 2 Peter states that the cosmos will be destroyed in a conflagration, an expectation shared by some ancient Jewish apocalyptic writings and by common Stoic cosmology.

A second response to the "scoffers" accuses them of misunderstanding God and God's purposes. Jesus' "coming" (2 Pet 3:4; cf. 1:16, 3:12) has not yet occurred because God is patient, not powerless. God desires for people to repent, and so God delays. When the time finally comes, however, arriving without warning like a thief (cf. Matt 24:42–44; Luke 12:39–40; 1 Thess 5:2; Rev 16:15), then God's judgment will happen. This judgment will disclose all things, which presumably includes the condemnation of the false teachers, as noted previously in the letter.

Second Peter presents frightful images of massive destruction with little explicit concern for the terror they might incite. Rather, the letter simply commends a life of "holiness and godliness" in which believers wait for and even accelerate God's timeline, presumably by encouraging others to repent while the opportunity remains (2 Pet 3:11–12). The audience's morality matters, according to 2 Peter, for believers must "strive to be found by [God] at peace" when all things come to an end. To give a final reminder that the Christian life should not be one of passivity or pretense, the letter returns to a familiar theme: it exhorts readers to "grow in the grace and knowledge" of Jesus Christ.

The Letter's Themes and Theological Emphases

The Parousia, Judgment, and Destruction

At its heart, 2 Peter consists of an extended grave exhortation to resist teachers and teachings that deviate from the traditions, practices, and moral standards associated with the apostles and their reliability as interpreters of Scripture and of God's intentions. The letter's theological rhetoric reiterates that God intends to punish sin and reward those who persevere in the truth. As it states its case, 2 Peter often looks toward the future, expecting that its audience's knowledge of what lies ahead will influence how they act in the present. The letter's specific expectations about the future convey a rather distinctive outlook on how believers might await the newness God will bring into being.

When 2 Peter warns about "scoffers" (2 Pet 3:3) who dismiss the possibility that Jesus will return and set creation on a new course, it indicates that Christ-followers in the early second century had come to new understandings about Jesus' next "coming," his *parousia* (2 Pet 1:16; 3:4, 12). According to the letter, the perceived delay in Jesus' return owes itself not to unreliability on God's part or mistaken interpretations on the apostles' part but to God's patience. God's desire for people's repentance keeps God from acting too hastily (2 Pet 3:9; cf. Acts 17:30–31, Joel 2:11–14). Furthermore, God's relationship to time differs from humanity's. As Ps 90:4 reveals in a poetic manner, one day and a thousand years, two radically different time spans for humans, are essentially equivalent for God (2 Pet 3:8). The mysterious and unknowable dimension of God's sense of timing does not excuse the church from vigilant expectation, however. Indeed, 2 Peter even indicates, and the letter is unique among the New Testament writings in stating the matter so plainly, that believers can hasten Christ's return either through their upright conduct or their efforts to usher others to repentance (2 Pet 3:11–12). Christ's extended absence thereby functions as a kind of motivational tactic for churches in this letter, a tactic that resonates with all of 2 Peter's strong warnings against moral and theological complacency. The author holds patient confidence in God in one hand and a life of urgent faithfulness and moral exertion in the other.

Other New Testament writings also link Christ's *parousia* with divine judgment and the punishment of God's adversaries, yet 2 Peter speaks additionally about the destruction of the heavens and the fiery melting of the universe's elements. Such an understanding of how the current world must end, as a precursor to the creation of "new heavens and a new earth," was familiar in ancient Stoic writings that described how the cosmos would be repristinated. It also recalls Old Testament passages in which fire serves as a metaphor for punishment inflicted by God (e.g., Deut 32:22; Isa 66:15–16; Zeph 1:18; Mal 4:1). Along with 2 Peter's basically dualistic outlook, the expectation of God triggering a future conflagration suggests that theological themes from Jewish apocalyptic writings also influenced the letter. In fact, 2 Peter expresses a rather exaggerated form of apocalypticism, for the book posits a very decisive break between the "present heavens and earth" (2 Pet 3:7) and a future existence (2 Pet 3:13). Because 2 Peter's imagery involves the world's incineration instead of its transformation or liberation, that break differs dramatically from other New Testament writings' expectations for the emergence of God's new age. The difference is especially important to highlight because 2 Peter's conception of a destroyed creation can lead to sweeping assumptions about the physical world. If the current plane of existence's allotted time is quickly running out and the physical world, its resources, and matter in general are doomed, then there is little incentive for the earth's inhabitants to prevent looming environmental and climatological catastrophe.

Some interpreters treat 2 Peter as a kind of obscure treasure trove of theological truths that appear only here. In other words, they take this book as a key place to learn about God's plans to see the world reborn out of a fiery destruction and the place that reveals the church's unique commission to accelerate the arrival of Christ's *parousia*. For other interpreters, including several leaders in the ancient church who considered 2 Peter an odd specimen, the book's unique perspectives make it an outlier within the conversations staged by the whole New Testament—one voice among many but hardly the dominant voice, and not a voice that can make its claims about creation or the *parousia* without encountering challenges from other New Testament voices that disagree. The extent to which Bible readers allow 2 Peter to inform their theology and ecology, as well as the strategies they use to put the book into conversation with other New Testament writings, have far-reaching ramifications for how Christian groups take a stand with regard to very important issues such as the nature of divine judgment, the church's efforts to promote justice and human flourishing, and the imperative to be responsible stewards of the earth.

Considering Difference in Christian Communities and in Theological Discourse

Although it is not the only New Testament writing to do so, 2 Peter exhibits a notable lack of tolerance toward differing theological positions and traditions. The letter takes an uncompromising approach toward differences, especially when it speaks about how believers should regard another who articulates faith differently from them or who is separate from their community of faith. Second Peter, much like its literary predecessor, Jude, distinguishes itself for its desire to keep its theological conversations limited to a restricted number of invited and approved guests.

Difference, or the existence of various perspectives in various Christian communities' beliefs and practices, was a major concern for many church leaders in the postapostolic age. The concern should evoke no surprise. Many movements, whether they are religious, political, or commercial, worry about losing members to rival groups and defending themselves against perceived threats, especially as movements grow larger, become more decentered, adapt to changing conditions, or see the departures of their most renowned leaders. The New Testament preserves a record of some of the worries that permeated early churches. Many of the General Letters, in particular, give voice to apprehensions about the influx of certain traditions. They usually counsel resistance and assail the reputations of other influential voices, which suggests that some Christian churches during the late first and early second centuries devoted substantial effort to preventing the loss of their members.

Various New Testament writings promote a range of strategies and manners of framing the questions when it comes to the issue of how to confront difference or newness. For example, some books say that the departure of members and friends from a fellowship reveals the true nature of those people, that they were really outsiders from the beginning (e.g., 1 John 2:19). By contrast, 2 Peter worries about genuine insiders straying away from the faith and as a result morphing into outsiders. In both cases authors are attempting to make theological sense of why Christian communities lose members or become divided. They consider who or what is at fault. They defend God's forbearance or threaten divine reprisals. They ask whether new ways of organizing communities or expressing "the faith" are wise or allowable. They attempt in various ways to counter the teachings, behaviors, and people they deem dangerous. They combat perceived threats with strategies such as reassurance, exhortation, reprimand, and warning.

The variety of strategies and the severity of the rhetoric in books like 2 Peter illustrate the complexity of the issues and the intensity they aroused in ancient Christian communities. Second Peter allows modern interpreters to witness an example of an author situated in the difficult position of trying to encourage and hold together Christian fellowships in a time when there were no manuals and few institutional structures to help the church do so. Being a part of those communities was, for many, a simultaneously boisterous, productive, yet fragile time of self-definition and theological reasoning. The liveliness had enduring and occasionally risky effects, for sometimes it resulted in the drawing of dividing lines that could not be easily erased and the inflicting of wounds that would never heal. Whether 2 Peter and its determination to maintain boundaries led to constructive outcomes or detrimental outcomes among its original audience is a judgment that modern interpreters cannot make with confidence.

How Christians should best engage difference and interpret their traditions in a changing landscape are questions that never go away. The New Testament has limitations in how it might inform those questions, since modern values about interfaith cooperation and ecumenical tolerance remain rather foreign to the biblical writings. But even so, the New Testament continues to exercise influence and even typifies some perennial forms of theological discourse. The stubborn assumptions and feisty rhetoric in books like 2 Peter recur and are probably necessary in certain but rare kinds of theological debates when possible outcomes are truly hazardous. But, and perhaps more commonly, those aspects of the letter also attract imitators who wield them in hurtful ways at inappropriate times. Throughout history the voices of Christian churches have sounded like 2 Peter's hostile and unyielding spirit probably more often than they should have. Modern interpreters of the New Testament are therefore not excused from deciding how they think 2 Peter and its sharp tones should or should not inform ways of thinking theologically and debating Christian self-identity in contemporary settings.

6

The Johannine Letters (1 John, 2 John, and 3 John)

All communities experience disagreement and conflict, whether it occurs among their members or between members and outsiders. All communities also need to determine how leadership will function in their midst in ways that promote a given group's purpose and identity. The inevitabilities of conflict and leadership relate to each other, for leaders often play critical roles in helping communities navigate the tricky ground of discerning when difference is healthy and salutary and when difference poses danger. Conflict, debate, and discernment manifest themselves and demand attention as young communities determine together who they are as they grow and change and as they attempt to maintain a particular identity for the long run. Christian communities in the first century of the church's existence were, of course, not immune.

Three related documents commonly referred to as the Johannine Letters—1 John, 2 John, and 3 John—allow Bible readers to observe a few dimensions of one or more ancient Christian communities' attempts to deal with dynamics of disagreement and leadership. The books come from a time when the church's apostolic era had passed away and Christian communities found themselves developing more formal and durable authority structures even as they continued to define and articulate their beliefs and practices. The three letters, especially 1 John, offer theological teaching about God and the Christian gospel, yet their principal concerns also include promoting Christian conduct and guarding orthodox beliefs against rival proposals. All three letters shine a light on one ancient author's attempt to address what he saw as threats to authentic Christian community, whether those threats stemmed from ideas capable of corrupting proper beliefs and practices, from people who opposed a community's leadership, or from both.

The books have a sectarian feel about them. They do not come from Christ-followers who insulated themselves from other Christ-followers in other regions or who cut off all contact with their unbelieving neighbors; the letters' sectarian quality shows itself instead in the concerns they address. Those concerns are almost exclusively internal, addressing how a community should function, what it should believe, and whom it should trust. In 1 John, for example, "we" and plural "you" language aligns repeatedly against "them"; even the syntax reinforces a separatist, fenced identity for the letter's audience. The rhetoric separates the audience from factions that appear to be part of the same community or associated communities, or maybe the groups had recently become separated from one another. The focus falls on community care; the letters barely address the question of how the members of a Christian community should relate to surrounding societies. The documents therefore do not come close to revealing the full spectrum of their author's and audience's understanding of what it means to be a Christ-follower. Neither do these short documents address the entire range of churches' experiences as they transitioned into the second century CE. Nevertheless, when the three letters describe struggle and conflict affecting a Christian community's ability to maintain its understanding of who it is, they can strike modern readers as timeless just as much as sectarian. For the most part, the conflicts and rivalries in these writings do not sound unfamiliar or uniquely ancient.

The Johannine Letters' sectarian tone does not make them coldhearted. They repeatedly refer to love as a central piece of God's character and the signal feature of Christian fellowship. Love therefore provides a measuring stick for appropriate behavior within Christian communities, even though the letters do not devote attention to what it might mean for their audience to love those who are not members. The emphasis on love—along with other theological themes such as "eternal life," "truth," and the incarnation of Jesus—makes the books resonate with the theology expressed in the Gospel according to John.

The Letters' Origins and Ancient Audience

The word *John* never appears in these books. Other than the mysterious name or title the author uses for himself in two places—"the elder"—the letters give no indication of who wrote them. Relatively early in church history, all three became associated with both the Gospel according to John and the Revelation to John, for some thought the same author was responsible for all five, and the author of Revelation identifies himself as "John" in multiple places. A number of other ancient Christian writers disagreed, with some of them insisting that the author of Revelation was not the source of the other four books, and others adding to that judgment their belief that the apostle John, the one they presumed to be the author of John, did not write the three shorter letters. On the whole, the linguistic and thematic trends of these books confirm the view that multiple authors bore responsibility for the five books. According to those trends there were at least three authors: the John who wrote Revelation, the unknown author—or perhaps multiple authors or revisers—of the Gospel according to John, and the unknown author of 1 John, 2 John, and 3 John. While some modern interpreters contend that 1 John may come from a different writer than 2 John and 3 John, the more persuasive arguments assert that all three of the Johannine Letters owe their existence to the same person: the unknown "elder," according to the way he designates himself in 2 John 1 and 3 John 1.

The striking thematic and theological similarities among the Gospel and these three short letters suggest that all four may have originally circulated in the same communities. It is likely that versions of John or the traditions that informed the Gospel were very well known to the author and first audience of 1 John, 2 John, and 3 John. It is also possible that the three letters, especially 1 John, address controversies that arose over how rightly to interpret the Gospel and its theological claims.

Investigations into the Gospel's and the letters' authorship have value because they call attention to the strong familial resemblance shared by these documents in their style, exhortations, and theological emphases. That resemblance encourages interpreters to consider similarities among the books, especially the letters. The prominent similarities and connections among the vocabulary and subject matter found in 1 John, 2 John, and 3 John suggest that all three originated around the same time to address the same general circumstances. All concern themselves with identifying what makes for a true believer and guarding against outside influences who teach different things, who resist the author's perspective, or who pose threats to a church's health and witness. Each letter has its own purpose: in 3 John, a personal letter in which the elder instructs a specific church leader, the author says he has "written something to the church" (3 John 9), which could be a reference to 2 John, which is a more public letter addressed to a Christian community as a whole. First John is not a letter, technically speaking, but a sermon or treatise. It may have been sent and delivered as a letter or attached as a supplement to 2 John or another letter. Possibly these three documents originally traveled together, allowing an authoritative figure, the elder, to instruct an individual church leader (3 John), to give pointed instructions to a wider congregation (2 John), and to address the community of faith with an extended theological treatise (1 John). Together, therefore, the Johannine Letters may represent an author's multipronged attempt to ensure that one or more Christian communities and their leaders would remain faithful to the author's vision for the church's proper theology and leadership structure.

Although the name frequently used to describe these three books, *the Johannine Letters,* distorts the picture by labeling 1 John as a letter, the expression remains here to stay. The designation honors the books' traditional association to an ancient teacher called John and acknowledges their thematic resonance with the Gospel according to John. The term also intentionally groups the three documents together as a way of highlighting their interactions with one another. Each one has a particular identity or message to communicate on its own, and together they tell a larger story about challenges faced in one congregation or a network of ancient Christian communities. It should be noted that assumptions about the value of reading the trio of letters in concert have never been uncontested. The writings of church leaders during the second through fourth centuries CE reveal that 1 John enjoyed much wider acceptance as an authoritative source for Christian faith and theology than the other two letters did. It took more time until Christian groups widely judged 2 John and 3 John as worthy of the same kind of esteem that 1 John attracted. Part of the reason for the delay was because those two books were not circulated as widely and vigorously as the more theologically rich and rhetorically powerful 1 John. Also, some ancient believers had lingering questions about who actually wrote 2 John and 3 John.

Reading the Johannine Letters together as a group still does not yield enough evidence to identify the author's or audiences' particular location and the precise time the documents were composed. Christian traditions that associate 1 John with the city of Ephesus cannot be confirmed or denied by material from the text itself. The letters' theological kinship with John suggests they were written after the Gospel. Their references to one or more schisms affecting their audience's Christian community indicate that some time passed between the writing of the Gospel and the writing of the letters. It is therefore reasonable to assume the letters were created within a decade either before or after 100 CE, although the question of their date does not need to exercise much influence on how one interprets them.

The author of the Johannine Letters claims to align himself with apostolic authority in 1 John 1:1–5, a passage that recalls aspects of the Gospel's prologue (John 1:1–18). Those opening lines of 1 John also refer to "the word of life," the message concerning Jesus, in ways similar to the Gospel's rhetoric about the incarnation of Jesus himself. With those verses the letters' author does not necessarily claim to be an apostle who knew Jesus face-to-face, but he does attempt to speak with the authority of traditions resonant with the Gospel and testimony about Jesus that was associated with the first generation of Christ-followers.

The elder who wrote the Johannine Letters stands on that apostolic authority to denounce teachings he deems heterodox and divisive (especially in 1 John and 2 John), yet he never unambiguously explains what those teachings are. When he accuses others of disobedience (1 John 2:4–6), he may merely attempt to discredit rival teachers or he could indicate that their teachings show outright contempt for the law or other ethical norms (cf. 1 John 2:9, 3:4). His references to those who deny "that Jesus is the Christ" (1 John 2:22; cf. 4:2) or "that Jesus Christ has come in the flesh" (2 John 7) appear to refer to teachings that either reject the idea that Jesus was truly a human being or draw complete distinctions between Jesus in his earthly ministry and the resurrected and glorified Christ, as if they were two separate beings. In 1 John 5:1–5, the elder suggests that other people's theological errors and ethical shortcomings are related.

Even after taking account of the assorted insights the letters offer into the author's appeals to authority and about the teachings he aims to denounce, still the precise nature of the purported false teachings remains ambiguous. Possibly the elder was not fully acquainted with what others were teaching, but more likely the ambiguity means he preferred to counter the falsehoods only by restating and reinforcing the ideas he held as orthodox. That strategy might have allowed him to avoid giving the ideas he detested the additional exposure they would have received if he made his case through a prolonged debate. As with most of the instances where the New Testament preserves evidence of disagreements in ancient churches, the Johannine Letters record only one side of the debate. The one-sidedness may frustrate researchers who want to reconstruct a more detailed history behind the letters and the communities they address, but it does not prevent the letters from making a case, albeit an abbreviated one, for a particular way of construing Christian existence and maintaining Christian community.

Overview of 1 John

Because 1 John weaves together various themes and often returns to subject matter it has previously addressed, it is difficult to map a progression of thought running through the letter. This does not mean it is haphazardly composed or lacks stylistic appeal. Although some interpreters hypothesize from 1 John's structure that it reflects various stages of authorship and editing, other explanations of the book's organization prove more convincing. Part of the book's rhetorical strength comes through those repetitions, especially when it repeatedly commends the audience. Furthermore, various sections of 1 John exhibit patterns or cadences that serve the book's ability to concentrate on specific messages and the book's efforts to make those messages especially memorable. Underlying the twists and turns of 1 John's literary architecture is a steady theological conviction that Jesus Christ embodies and discloses God and God's characteristics. In Jesus, people *experience* God.

To experience God is to experience love, truth, light, and life. Readers learn this through 1 John's fondness for dualisms. Resembling the Gospel according to John in this regard, frequently 1 John strikes contrasts between pairs of opposites such as light and darkness, love and hatred, life and death, and truth and falsehood. It locates a pair's positive element in God's nature and activity, resulting in believers' ability to share in that thing or to "walk" (1 John 1:6; 2:6, 11; cf. 2 John 4, 6; 3 John 3) accordingly in life. God is light (1 John 1:5) and has made light shine in the shadows so believers can likewise be in the light (1 John 1:7; 2:8–10). God is love (1 John 4:8, 16), and this love becomes manifest in believers' obedience, which shows they know and abide in God (1 John 4:7, 16; 5:3). God's gift of eternal life resides in Jesus the Son (1 John 5:11), who himself is "the true God and eternal life" (1 John 5:20). As a result, with the advent of this eternal life believers know now that they "have passed from death to life" (1 John 3:14). First John refers to the Spirit as "the truth" (1 John 5:6; cf. 4:6), although it is not fully clear whether 1 John focuses specifically on the Holy Spirit (cf. John 15:26–27), a more impersonal notion of "the spirit" as the living and active testimony about Jesus, or the force and vitality of believers' identification with God. In any case, the book sees "the truth" (1 John 1:8; 2:4, 21; 3:19; 5:6) manifest in God's interaction with humanity. Believers likewise become fully associated with the truth (1 John 3:19) and exist "in him who is true"—namely, Jesus Christ (1 John 5:20).

Another pairing, the opposition of antichrists to Jesus Christ, discloses some of what motivates this book's sense of urgency. The New Testament refers to "antichrist(s)" only four times: in 1 John 2:18, 22; 4:3; and 2 John 7. Those passages have no connection at all to the beast described in Rev 13:11–18, whom popular interpretations, following some ancient interpreters' lead, have erroneously dubbed *the* antichrist. Instead, the antichrists in 1 John are people who have separated themselves from the audience's community and teach erroneous things about Jesus and his work on earth "in the flesh" (1 John 4:1–3; cf. 2:18–23). The author ventures very serious claims about those secessionists or outcasts, declaring that they belong to the world and not to God (1 John 4:4–6) and that their departure from the community reveals not only the falseness of their teaching but also that previously they did not really "belong to us" (1 John 2:19). The author sees no middle ground or room for compromise regarding them.

The threat of the antichrists and their false teaching provides occasion for a warning about the arrival of "the last hour" (1 John 2:18), a reference to "the day of judgment" (1 John 4:17; cf. 2 John 8), and an expectation of Jesus' future "coming"—his *parousia* in Greek—when he will be revealed (1 John 2:28, 3:2). Those parts of the book that anticipate a specific future consummation of God's plan, culminating in judgment, represent ways that 1 John's theological emphases occasionally diverge from those in the Gospel according to John. The Gospel has much less to say about a coming judgment and hardly anything explicit to say about Jesus' return.

Despite the warnings it issues to its readers, 1 John maintains a dominant tone of encouragement. It reminds believers about the eternal life they possess (1 John 5:13; cf. John 20:31). The author urges his audience to love one another, thereby obeying Jesus' commandment to do so (1 John 3:11–16, 23; 4:7–11; cf. 2 John 5–6; John 13:34; 15:12, 17). He reassures them that Jesus cleanses them from their sins, and he commends confessing sins (1 John 1:8–10; 5:16). At the same time, and perhaps incongruously with the book's exhortations about confession, 1 John claims that those who abide in Jesus Christ cannot commit sins (1 John 3:4–10; 5:18; cf. 3 John 11). With that claim the letter likely aims to emphasize the transformational nature of a life lived with Christ. True believers, the author insists, abide; they remain connected to Christ and to his love. That manner of abiding means to live not only in conformity to Jesus' life but also, first of all, in an intimate, secure relationship with him—a relationship in which one's life becomes subsumed by Jesus' identity as God's Son (1 John 5:20; cf. 2:22–24; 4:9).

Overview of 2 John

This letter from "the elder" addresses an unknown "elect lady and her children," which probably indicates a distinct congregation of Christ-followers, although some interpreters speculate the "elect" or "chosen" addressee might have referred to an actual person, a woman who was the recognized leader of one or more Christian communities (cf. 2 John 13). The letter begins by commending the people whose way of life demonstrates they are "walking in the truth," and it instructs them about a familiar commandment: to "love one another" (2 John 5; cf. 1 John 3:11–16, 23; 4:7–11; John 13:34; 15:12, 17). The author quickly turns to warn readers about "deceivers," specifically those who have "gone out into the world" (2 John 7; cf. 1 John 4:1). That image of going out, considered in light of 1 John's references to false teachers who had previously been in close fellowship with the book's audience (1 John 2:19; cf. 4:1), indicates that the deceivers were once members of the elect lady's community. They deceive because they "do not confess that Jesus Christ has come in the flesh" (2 John 7). Any such person opposes Christ and earns the label *the antichrist*, which refers to a person whose position or conduct stands in utter contrast to those who "abide in the teaching of Christ" (2 John 9). Because of this firm distinction, the church should refuse hospitality to the antichrists, lest the church's members become coparticipants in the "evil deeds" of those deceitful outsiders (2 John 10–11).

Overview of 3 John

"The elder" writes a personal and affectionate letter to a friend, an otherwise unknown man named Gaius. The letter commends Gaius for his "faithfulness to the truth" and for the love and support he shows to other believers, even though they once were strangers to him (3 John 3, 5–6). Next, the elder expresses consternation about another man: Diotrephes, about whom also nothing else is known. Concerns about false doctrines and separatist "antichrists," so prominent in 1 John and 2 John, do not appear in this letter. Instead, the elder takes issue with Diotrephes in 3 John because of his conduct: he resists the elder's wishes and authority.

Diotrephes possesses significant influence among the believers known to the author and to Gaius, for he forbids some of the author's associates from receiving hospitality in a Christian community and even casts them out of the church's fellowship. The letter complains that Diotrephes "likes to put himself first" and does not honor Gaius and the elder's authority but instead circulates "false charges" against them (3 John 9–10). The elder adds a brief commendation of someone named Demetrius. All the references to various people and their conflicts suggest the letter originally came from a situation in which various church leaders were publically disagreeing about an authority structure and possibly also about the proper practical management of one or more Christian congregations. Even though the precise details of the conflict remain unascertainable in such a brief document, the letter serves as the elder's attempt to reassert his authority among a congregation or collection of congregations, to maintain his relationships or alliances with Gaius and Demetrius, and to make clear his impatience with Diotrephes.

The Letters' Themes and Theological Emphases

Love

All of the Johannine Letters speak frequently of "love." Christian identity, they insist, depends on love, understood in two different but complementary ways. First, God is the source of love; indeed, "God is love" (1 John 4:8, 16), meaning that God's love is a defining characteristic of God's own being and activity. Jesus, as the Father's Son, likewise participates in God's truth and love (2 John 3). Further, Jesus makes God's love known by giving his life on behalf of others (1 John 3:16, 4:10), thereby cleansing and forgiving sins (1 John 1:7, 2:12).

The second dimension of love, as the letters describe it, is its definitive role in Christian fellowship. Love among believers constitutes the essential mark of the new existence they enjoy from God. Conversely, those who do not love their spiritual siblings prove themselves to be "children of the devil" (1 John 3:10). Two of the letters therefore restate the "new commandment" Jesus gives to believers in John: "love one another" (John 13:34–35; 15:12, 17; 1 John 3:11–16, 23; 4:7–11; 2 John 5). Furthermore, in 3 John 1, the elder speaks of his relationship with Gaius as one characterized by mutual love. As in John, the letters confine their focus on loving one another to love that believers share with others within the community of faith. The Johannine Letters give little if any encouragement to their readers to love those in the wider world in similar ways. If the letters' notion of intramural love can also make God's love for the whole world manifest through lifestyle and the witness of Christian communities, as Jesus suggests in John 13:34–35, the letters do not contemplate the possibility.

By associating two aspects of love—love as a core characteristic of God and as the sure mark of authentic Christian community—the Johannine Letters describe love and the obligation to love others as theological notions. In other words, the author encourages readers to love one another because doing so is an expression of theological realities—because God, who is love, makes mutual love possible. God does this not by issuing commands but by having entered the world, a hostile territory where "the evil one" exercises power (1 John 5:19), and by having lived and died there, for the sake of the world. Insofar as the letters, especially 1 John and 2 John, emphasize Jesus' bodily existence, they do not permit their audience to comprehend love as an abstract moral or ethical category. Rather, love is an effective, active expression. God *demonstrated* love in the flesh, through the incarnation. Love was manifest also in the incarnate Jesus' willingness to give his life to benefit others and to remove the power of sins and the blemishes sins inflict. To love one another therefore requires believers to display the same kind of presence and commitment among one another. The existential and self-giving character of such love surpasses warm feelings or good wishes.

Leadership and Schism

The New Testament, as a collection of diverse writings from different times and places, refers to and commends different forms of leadership operating in different Christian communities. Various books use an assortment of terms to name leaders and offices. Various authors speak differently about their own authority or address others' authority in distinctive ways. Various details emerge about the decisions and controversies the early churches had to navigate. In the particular case of the Johannine Letters, the books reveal very little about the author's specific authority over or within the communities he addresses. He may have enjoyed an extensive and widely recognized authority, or he may have written the letters to gain leverage in a more contested environment. In each book, however, he clearly seeks to reassert and exercise authority. Whatever were the precise historical circumstances surrounding these documents, the letters obviously bear the residue of tensions present in early Christian communities' attempts to navigate real organizational and structural difficulties. Whether the elder who wrote the letters was an influential or a marginal voice in his corner of the ancient Christian church, his writings touch on timeless questions: What qualifies as religious authority, and how should churches confer, exercise, and heed it?

A variety of specific issues bubble up from the letters' rhetoric as the author contends for certain ways of believing, living, and treating divergent opinions. The elder appeals to the authority of traditions and longstanding convictions or beliefs. Aside from an explicit mention of Cain in 1 John 3:12, the author's arguments rely on only very subtle and infrequent allusions to scriptural texts or themes (e.g., 1 John 2:11 and Isa 6:10). He chooses also to invoke a sense of authority inherent in a church office or in his general reputation, desired or actual, when he speaks of himself as "the elder" and others as "co-workers" (3 John 8). He sees value and a kind of intrinsic authority in the presence of unity and mutual love among believers. In the end, the author's multipronged appeals to authority provide him a warrant to issue stark judgments to his audience. He uses his platform to promote and enforce his notion of orthodox beliefs. In one case, his dedication to orthodoxy leads him to tell his audience to deny hospitality to others whom he considers negative influences (2 John 10–11).

The letters' sectarian rhetoric spoke about and likely exacerbated divisions in ancient settings. It has continued to make divisions across the long span of church history. The strong statements about "antichrist(s)" and the elder's unyielding criticisms of people who have separated themselves from the original audience's community strike many modern people as unduly harsh and intolerant. By contrast, some Christians treat the letters' rhetoric as a warrant for their own desires to draw indelible borders between themselves and their theological rivals. Any assessment of the letters needs to consider how they might have functioned in their original setting. They reveal very few specific details about the theological falsehoods and ethical failings the author aimed to expose, but obviously he saw them as a clear and present danger to congregations. The elder's eagerness to draw impermeable boundaries between truth and falsehood spotlights a persistent challenge Christ-followers faced especially during their first centuries of existence: how to determine when an issue of belief or behavior is so foundational that disagreement about it provides justification for severing fellowship with another group.

Groups of many kinds define themselves by making decisions about what it means for people to belong to them. Not every attempt to maintain separations between a community's insiders and outsiders must be destructive or polemical, but certainly some turn out that way. The elder's attitudes toward the schisms his audience were experiencing could have arisen from grudges and an angry or immature unwillingness even to listen to divergent points of view. His words could have resonated very differently, however, if the letters were his attempt to protect vulnerable communities that were being harmed by abusive people or patently dangerous teachings. Any appraisal of the elder's strategies and rhetoric, and also his motivations, has to depend on what interpreters imagine was the nature of the threats and falsehoods he sought to combat. Not all threats and falsehoods are what they appear to be; nor are all the same.

Embodied Love

The letters' impassioned warnings against false teaching represent more than turf wars waged among aggrieved leaders. Disputes about

Jesus reside beneath the letters' deep concerns. Those who deny that Jesus Christ "has come in the flesh" (1 John 4:2; 2 John 7; cf. 1 John 2:22) receive strong criticism, yet the author never explains exactly what those theological foes believed. The issue evidently revolved around the question of whether Jesus was a real human being or around the question of whether Jesus' identity as the Christ and his role in salvation were part and parcel of his humanity. Those who departed or were barred from the community or communities that received these letters likely understood Jesus as a purely spiritual revelation of God, or they considered salvation as pertaining to a distinctively spiritual and nonphysical, disembodied existence. If the elder was accurately representing the other group's views, then he apparently was contending against rudimentary expressions of what would eventually become known as Docetism. Docetism refers to a family of theological movements that asserted that Jesus only appeared to possess a true human body. Well into the second century CE, docetic ideas played a part in the flourishing of gnostic theologies in numerous Christian circles. Many in the church opposed those ideas for various reasons, especially because docetic theologies rendered Jesus' crucifixion as an illusion or as unconnected to the salvation he makes possible.

The Johannine Letters, much like John, articulate a decidedly nondocetic theology, for the books perceive deep implications in understanding Jesus as an embodied expression—a truly flesh-and-blood realization—of God's love and presence. One such implication of God's appearance in human flesh is that forgiveness and a new life marked by love and a promise of sinlessness become available to believers now, as they live their own embodied existence. Salvation, then, has consequences and benefits that are available immediately and that affect human lives and relationships.

The author of the letters may have feared that neglecting the reality of Jesus' humanity would transform Christian religion into a spiritual flight from embodied and social living. That kind of flight could have negative consequences for people's physical and material well-being, especially if those consequences squelch believers' regard and care for those who suffer from illness, poverty, or exclusion. Even if the elder did not draw exactly those same conclusions about the negative consequences of docetic claims about Jesus Christ, Christian theologians have done so at various points in the church's history. In recent decades some interpreters have noted that taking seriously salvation's ramifications for human bodies matters thoroughly for Christians' efforts to think more expansively and holistically about Christianity's ability to speak good news about issues pertaining to gender, economics, ethnicity, colonialism, sexuality, and disability. The Johannine Letters may have had their origins in localized skirmishes over leadership and the contours of acceptable teachings. Their most durable and precious contributions to Christian belief and practice, however, probably reside in their insistent and generative claim that applies in any setting: Christian faith is about participating in divine, embodied love. That participation, the letters assert, allows for the transformation of human existence now, not in a far-off future.

7

The Letter of Jude

A persistent misrepresentation of the Bible holds that the Old Testament brims with descriptions of divine wrath whereas the New Testament dedicates itself to testifying about God's willingness to forgo wrath in favor of showing mercy. Those who assume the truth of that simplistic and thoroughly flawed characterization should spend time with Jude. Jude does not deny or refuse to celebrate the reality of God's grace. Yet this short letter devotes much more of its attention to promising, with an unyielding confidence mixed with a large dose of scorn, that God will punish those who are disobedient. Numerous events and prophecies recorded in the Jewish Scriptures and other revered Jewish writings remain instructive for understanding the severe consequences of disregarding God's demands, according to Jude. Those familiar traditions establish that God has rarely been loath to judge and punish people, including those who had good reason to know better than to disrespect divine authority. The stories to which Jude refers imply that God remains ready to judge rebelliousness and immorality even after the advent of Jesus Christ.

With stern rhetoric that expresses deep concern about the corrosive influence of certain unidentified teachings and ways of living, Jude reaffirms that God is a merciful Savior who works through Jesus Christ. The letter simultaneously expresses little patience with those who would presume that divine mercy grants them the freedom to stray from God's appointed ways. Jude insists that God's judgment and the punishment that follow from it are not incompatible with God's mercy.

The Letter's Origins and Ancient Audience

As with the other General Letters, Jude does not define its audience with precision. It addresses itself widely to "those who are called, who are beloved in God the Father and kept safe for Jesus Christ" (Jude 1), without specifying where they might have resided. Because of the letter's brevity, it contains very few clues to indicate what kind of believers the author sought to address and even fewer clues to grant insight into their specific circumstances. Pointed criticism of "intruders," "dreamers," slanderers, and divisive people give reason to assume that the book's original audiences were members of Christian communities beset by controversies over leadership, correct teachings, and appropriate ways of living. The letter's primary strategy for encouraging those readers is to draw firm lines of demarcation between them and the corrupt "intruders."

In many ways Jude serves as a monument, albeit a brief and undetailed one, to the struggles some Christ-followers experienced in trying to determine how to interact with other professed believers who disagreed with them. From Jude's perspective, the solution to those struggles was rather cut-and-dried: faithful living means adhering to received traditions. As for those who disagreed, either because they taught and lived the Christian faith differently or because they willingly transgressed certain moral standards, Jude says they deserve rebuke, for God will surely judge their rebelliousness.

With only a handful of sentences, Jude makes its case while displaying familiarity with Jewish Scriptures. It cites the exodus from Egypt and names Sodom, Gomorrah, Cain, Balaam, and Korah. It includes references and allusions to at least two extrabiblical documents: 1 Enoch and another Jewish writing, probably the Testament of Moses. The interaction with traditions preserved in Jewish Scriptures and other influential Jewish texts does not prove that the audience comprised only Jewish and not gentile Christ-followers, but it does suggest an audience—as well as an author—deeply committed to the ongoing value and validity of Jewish theological traditions.

The Question of Authorship

According to Christian traditions that originated in antiquity, one of Jesus' brothers or half-brothers, a man named Jude, wrote the letter. This rather common ancient name, which Jude 1 uses to identify the book's attributed author, could also be translated as "Judas," as it is in other parts of the New Testament. The particular man named by the letter has been remembered as "Jude" primarily to distinguish him from Judas Iscariot and various others named Judas in biblical writings (e.g., Matt 10:4; Luke 6:16; Acts 5:37, 9:11, 15:22; 1 Macc 2:4). In two places where the New Testament refers to Jesus' brothers by name, one of them is called Jude/Judas. English translations typically refer to him as "Judas" in those passages (see Matt 13:55, Mark 6:3; cf. Acts 1:13, 1 Cor 9:5), however, even though the Greek name is the same as what appears in Jude 1.

The letter identifies this "Jude" as Jesus' "slave" (rendered politely but misleadingly in the NRSV as "servant") and as the "brother of James" (Jude 1), presumably the James who was also related to Jesus and was a onetime and influential leader of the young church in Jerusalem (Acts 12:17; 15:13; 21:18; Gal 1:19; 2:9, 12). If indeed one of Jesus' own contemporaries or family members wrote Jude, then it likely was written around the middle of the first century CE. Evidence strongly suggests, however, that someone else wrote Jude as a pseudepigraphic letter, perhaps closer to the end of the first century.

Because history did not preserve any writings from the pen of Jude the brother of Jesus that might be scrutinized alongside this book, it is impossible to analyze the authorship question by comparing the letter's vocabulary and theological themes to other documents. A careful reading of Jude reveals, however, two other things to learn about the book's writer. First, whoever wrote the letter possessed a relatively sophisticated command of Greek; the writing style is more refined than most of the books in the New Testament, although it still falls far short of erudite when compared to other Hellenistic authors. Many interpreters consider it unlikely that one of Jesus' brothers from a town in Galilee would have acquired such literary skill, casting doubt on whether that actual man named Jude could have written the document without assistance. Additionally, it is easy to imagine why an anonymous Christian author might be eager to attribute his writing to the name and legacy of someone who was closely connected to Jesus during his life. Such a connection might have enhanced the document's authority, especially in Jude's multiple appeals to the apostles and those it calls "the saints" who reliably held Christian tradition in trust, creating a foundation on which later believers could faithfully stand (Jude 3, 17–18, 20, 24). No matter who wrote the letter, its literary associations with one of Jesus' siblings potentially strengthens the book's argument when it attempts to reinforce the importance of established teachings and practices. Those associations might have helped the book persuade an audience that was facing pressures to embrace other doctrines, to follow new leaders, or to ally themselves with other Christ-followers who held differing beliefs.

Because Jude is so concise, thoroughly persuasive arguments about its authorship remain impossible to generate, whether those arguments contend for a pseudepigraphic letter or a document originally written by one of Jesus' relatives. In the end, the debates are not very consequential for interpreting this short book and understanding the basic argument it made to its original audience. If Jude is a pseudepigraphic letter, even then interpreters can discern next to nothing about the book's actual author. Like other General Letters, especially James and 1 Peter, Jude makes no extended effort to capitalize on its attributed author's authority, exemplary personal conduct, privileged knowledge, or unique experiences. The literary persona of the historical man Jude, Jesus' brother or half-brother, proves to be largely irrelevant to the letter's exhortations. The book at its beginning simply names Jude, a man about whom virtually nothing is known from other early Christian writings, and then he drops out of sight.

Overview

Jude initially presents itself as a letter, for it includes a standard salutation. The rest of the book, however, reads more like a sermon, entreating an audience to remain faithful through stern warnings about the perils they face and concluding in Jude 24–25 with a stirring benediction that ascribes glory to God.

With a salutation that invokes the name and memory of Jude, the letter subtly recalls the era and witness of Jesus' original apostles, people whom Jesus' brother Jude/Judas knew, even if he himself was not one of the Twelve. Immediately following the salutation, the letter states its intentions quite plainly. It urges its audience "to contend for the faith that was once for all entrusted to the saints" (Jude 3). The language ascribes a static or settled character to "the faith" (cf. Col 1:23, 2:7; 1 Tim 4:1; 6:10, 21; 2 Tim 4:7; Titus 1:4; 2 Pet 1:1). Such a way of speaking implies that the saints—that is, Christ-followers—hold and have held authentic Christian teaching in their care, as its appointed guardians. Jude's readers should therefore know that they have neither the freedom nor the responsibility to reinterpret or revise doctrine. Nor can they live however they choose. Rather, the audience should preserve the teachings and traditions that are as old as Jesus' original apostles. Jude thereby coaxes its readers while it also discredits people who it thinks "pervert" the true faith (Jude 4). The letter describes those foes as outsiders and shifty, for they are "intruders" who operate furtively, concealing their true motives. They aim to change the established faith into something it is not.

Jude never names the "intruders" or restates their specific beliefs. Repeatedly, however, the letter associates them with "licentiousness," "sexual immorality," self-serving ambitions, and the utter absence of moral self-control. Many interpreters take those criticisms to indicate that Jude takes aim against people who abuse God's grace by living an openly libertine lifestyle. In other words, the "intruders" may have assumed that the abundance of God's mercy means there will be no repercussions for immoral behavior (cf. Rom 6:1–2). Interpreters of Jude need to note, however, that in Greco-Roman society accusations of moral depravity were a relatively standard rhetorical weapon to use against teachers that an accuser considered false or unorthodox, no matter what the specific nature of their teachings was. It was common among both Jews and gentiles to accuse one's ideological enemies of divisive and morally repugnant behavior. Jude may therefore be preferring to smear the "intruders" rather than debate their ideas. There must have been much more to their teachings, although it cannot be determined from the letter alone.

To demonstrate the foolishness and theological ignorance of those who flout God's resolve to judge disobedience, the letter looks to Jewish traditions. God wiped out some of those whom God had previously saved from slavery in Egypt (e.g., Num 14:26–45, Exod 32:1–29). God punished insubordinate angels who defied God's design by mating with human women, according to The Book of the Watchers, a Jewish apocalyptic writing that became a part of the document 1 Enoch (cf. Gen 6:1–4). God also destroyed Sodom and Gomorrah because of their residents' similar manner of sexual immorality. In particular, the reference to what the NRSV renders as "unnatural lust" in Jude 7 refers to the men of Sodom's deviant desire to commit sexual intercourse specifically with angelic beings (Gen 19:1–29). The implication is that a human being's desire to copulate with angels contravenes the way God has ordered the cosmos with its separate inhabitants.

Jude also castigates the intruders who imperil the letter's audience, calling them deluded "dreamers" (Jude 8) who reject the authority of God and responsible leaders. They fail to recognize what the archangel Michael knew—that the Lord alone, and not he, possesses the right and jurisdiction to execute judgment (citing a story about Michael and the devil that was probably once part of the Jewish writing the Testament of Moses). The dangerous people whom Jude indicts resemble other rebellious figures whose actions led to violence and their own destruction: Cain (Gen 4:1–16), Balaam (Num 31:1–20; cf. Num 25:1–9; Rev 2:14), and Korah (Num 16). The villains of the letter are therefore utterly out of step with God's purposes and bound for judgment. Like clouds that produce no rain and trees that fail to bear fruit, these intruders do not cooperate with what God intends. The prophecy about God's intention to judge sinners recorded in 1 En. 1:9 applies to people like them, for there will be severe consequences for their ungodliness (Jude 14–15).

The letter has very little to say about Jesus Christ and his specific role or effects regarding the anticipated divine judgment. The presence and influence of intruders nevertheless reaffirms the reliability of the apostles whom Jesus chose, for the apostles' teachings and legacy preserve the truth and create a trustworthy tradition, as proved by the apostles' correct predictions about the eventual emergence of "scoffers" (Jude 18). As for Jesus Christ himself, his mercy continues to be the source of eternal life. The book's attention to judgment does not eclipse the reality of mercy. Christ's mercy likewise motivates his followers to treat others mercifully. The disobedient and immoral people of this world are not beyond hope, although the letter's audience should minister to these people carefully and with an awareness that ungodly people can be a virulent source of contamination. Such people defile whatever comes near to them, even their clothing (Jude 23).

The Letter's Themes and Theological Emphases

Jewish Theological Traditions

To support its stern condemnations, Jude recalls several stories and assurances recorded in writings from Jewish history. Various texts bear witness to the moral structure God has ordained and to God's history of judging those who act disobediently. Jude's argument endures as a prominent example of a New Testament writing's heavy reliance on existing theological traditions in its efforts to articulate a Christian perspective on God and God's engagement with humanity. Jude draws freely on a modest variety of Jewish traditions in its efforts to teach its audience about God, exhorting them in light of God's determination to punish disobedience. Jesus Christ may play a decisive role in Jude's theological outlook, even if the book does not say much about Jesus, but neither Jesus nor his deeds make irrelevant the older testimonies about God and about the nature of faithfulness to God.

The letter makes use of stories from the Torah and material from the Testament of Moses and 1 Enoch. Jude has concerned some Christian readers over the centuries because it refers to all of this material as equally authoritative, even though the Testament of Moses and 1 Enoch never finally found their way into the formal canons of the Jewish Tanakh and the Christian Old Testament. Those concerns about Jude's influences belong to periods of time after Jude was written, once Jewish and Christian groups started to define "Scripture" as a more exclusive and defined set of texts and spoke of those texts' unique authority as primary sources of theological knowledge. It appears that the author of Jude assumed the letter's audience would hardly disapprove of what those two ancient apocalyptic writings have to say about God. After all, their general worldview and depiction of God resonate with the apocalyptic-theological momentum that travels through most of the books in the New Testament. The early currents of Christian theology were fed by multiple streams of tradition. What qualified as legitimate sources of theological authority was hardly an obvious or settled question during the earliest centuries of the Christian churches.

Combative Rhetoric and Preserving Orthodoxy

It is not terribly difficult to trace what fuels Jude's theological perspective, even though that perspective comes across only in bits and pieces. Jude holds that God has established a particular cosmological and moral order that must be respected by human beings and angels alike. God calls people and angels to occupy certain positions within that order (e.g., Jude 1, 6–7, 8, 12–13, 21, 24). Those who violate those arrangements show contempt for God, which is the basis for Jude's understanding of immorality and rebelliousness, whether waged against God or against "the faith." Jude's view of the moral order does not prove that the people whom the letter labels "intruders" were actually bad apples, but it serves as the letter's warrant to state without reservation that divine judgment certainly awaits them.

Although Jude does not include a detailed description of judgment's consequences, it nevertheless provides summaries with grim terms: "condemnation," "a punishment of eternal fire," "deepest darkness," and "the fire" (Jude 4, 7, 13, 23). By depicting the intruders' waywardness as contagious, the letter implies that the disorderliness of their moral conduct now, on this side of God's certain judgment, corrupts authentic Christian fellowship and worship. The author's desire to protect Christian communities and their beliefs derives, therefore, from a desire to honor the order he believes God has established. For that reason Jude suggests the intruders should be excluded from the audience's celebration of the Lord's Supper at communal meals, called "love-feasts" (Jude 12; cf. 1 Cor 11:17–32). Jude's theology leads to an understanding of Christian identity and fellowship in which separation looks more desirable than solidarity under certain circumstances.

Jude articulates its theological perspective with a pronounced polemical accent. The letter's tone does not make Jude unique among the New Testament writings. The Johannine Letters also draw unyielding distinctions among groups in attempts to promote and preserve what the letters consider to be right teachings. Second Peter, a book that drew much of its material from Jude, also has its moments of fury directed at people it deems false and dangerous. Jude uses sharp rhetoric to support its case about what constitutes true Christian belief and practice. Those kinds of debates would continue within Christian communities well beyond Jude's original setting, into the second and third centuries, with even greater polemical ferocity. In some respects, debates over what makes for authentic Christian beliefs and behavior have never ended but only evolved as Christianity has grown and developed over time. The work of determining what constitutes acceptable or deviant theology never goes away, as Jude reminds Christian readers. Multiple options nevertheless remain for how modern Christians choose to conduct this work and for the charity and tone that they might employ.

The anger that magnifies Jude's criticism of the "intruders" conveys the seriousness with which the letter views the situation, even though Jude does not provide enough information to reconstruct what were the specific points of disagreement. For some reason, Jude expresses little interest in commending forbearance or constructive dialogue. Jude prefers to assail opponents' character and to stigmatize their ideas as dangerous innovations rather than to hold their actual beliefs up for a measured analysis. Such serious speech and unspecific criticisms have repeatedly throughout the history of the Bible's interpretation attracted those in the Christian church who would carelessly imitate that brand of rhetoric. Also, the letter's warnings about "condemnation" and "eternal fire" have encouraged many to adopt terroristic theatrics as an evangelistic tool or to wield mercilessly narrow definitions of orthodoxy to weed dissonant voices out of Christian communities. The book's moral and theological outrage gets reincarnated when Christians use Jude, or act as if indirectly inspired by it, in their eagerness to denounce and damage those who believe or live differently.

Because it is impossible to know the reasons behind the letter's belligerent approach, interpreters need to take care not to assume their responsibility is as simplistic as trying to read the minds and motives of ancient people by imputing malice on either the author as a frightened and angry man or those he criticizes so severely as obviously unethical degenerates. Interpretations of Jude would understand the letter in a particular way if interpreters could know with certainty that it was written to stifle every ounce of dissent among anyone who dared to disagree with an authoritarian author. Alternatively, interpretations would assess Jude's rhetoric quite differently if interpreters knew the letter was written to Christian communities that were being bullied and torn apart by abusive interlopers or moral monsters. Other interpretive conclusions are possible, of course, and entertaining those options about the letter and its possible setting can alter the message one hears in Jude. In any case, Christians do well to resist the temptation to imitate Jude's combative and contemptuous rhetoric when they cannot determine exactly what purpose it might have served in the first place.

Jude's unyielding posture shocks many modern readers. Yet when Jude advocates separation and resists any inclination to compromise, it is hardly the only volume in the New Testament to do so. But Jude and most of the other biblical books with such rigid perspectives do not base their views on a desire to pursue ideological purity as the greatest good. Jude's author, for example, may actually have been more concerned about bolstering the church's chances for longevity than about zealously defending an orthodoxy, even though he regards the latter as something that will guarantee the former. At its core Jude expresses an earnest concern for churches' survival.

The overall evidence from much of the New Testament reveals that numerous Christian leaders writing near the end of the first century considered themselves living in an era fraught with peril. They viewed Christian communities as vulnerable and the power of the gospel in danger of becoming diluted or lost. Interpreters ought not to pass judgment on a particular book's strategies for protecting a Christian community during that era without also considering what exactly an ancient author thought was so threatening to the church. As for Jude, it exhibits a relatively narrow range of vision toward what it considers to be corrosive influences; it does not specify what it opposes. Other New Testament writings, however, speak more descriptively about larger and more systemic dangers facing Christian communities. The book that follows Jude, Revelation, offers a good example. Revelation has much to say about the certainty of divine judgment, the horrific punishments that await some, the need for believers to persevere, and the perils that beset Christ-followers. Perhaps if Jude was, like Revelation, more specific about the virulent nature of the various things that might threaten Christian communities and the distinctiveness of the Christian witness, maybe Jude's fierce and take-no-prisoners resolve to protect certain expressions of Christian identity would appear more compassionate and less reactionary. The point is not necessarily to force other New Testament writings always to trump what Jude has to say; rather, it is to remember that Jude represents only one voice among several that still speak from the sometimes turbulent first century of the Christian church's existence.

8

The Revelation to John

Revelation is a book of extremes. It describes both freakish and glorious visions that tell of widespread desolation and also lasting restoration. The book issues grave threats on one page and promises bountiful succor on the next. It tells of rampaging arrogance and also vulnerable humility. The book's catalog of images range from a pool of burning sulfur to a spring of refreshing water. Its portraits of God and divine activity evoke horror as well as praise.

Stretched to the limits by all the extremes and persistent fierce conflict, the universe finds itself at a breaking point in the stories Revelation tells. Nations inflict and suffer destruction, celestial bodies undergo portentous transformations, and heavenly forces wage battles until all of God's opponents in heaven and on earth experience ultimate defeat. Everything will undergo dramatic change, according to the cosmic secrets Revelation divulges to its readers. The prospect of so much transformation, as Revelation presents it, aims to help Christ-followers keep their bearings and not fall prey to panic. The book means to tell the truth to believers who lived in a Roman province, generating confidence among them while also gravely exhorting them toward faithful living in dangerous circumstances.

As its title suggests, Revelation is about seeing and discovering. It allows its audience to peer into an alternate existence. The book speaks from a heavenly point of view, from a vantage point in which angels, deceased believers, Satan (depicted as a dragon), Jesus Christ (depicted most often as a lamb), and even the enthroned God can be seen. Given the book's peculiar point of view, some aspects come across as disorienting or convoluted. On one hand, parts of Revelation employ a basic narrative structure; various figures speak and act in various settings. On the other hand, the action does not necessarily follow a clear trajectory of obvious narrative sequence or causes and effects. The flow and pacing of the events the book alleges to reveal come off as deliberately vague, and the narration proceeds more cyclically than chronologically. Furthermore, the theological rhetoric of Revelation is awash with symbolism, which adds to the interpretive challenges and enhances the book's capacity to stir up imaginations through the power of metaphor.

No other New Testament writing can match Revelation's arcane character. Yet the book does not serve as an escapist's manifesto; it may peer into unearthly places and celebrate the mysterious character of God's plans, but it does not call its audience to reject their current habitat or to devalue their current existence as they hope for a better one. The mysteries serve Revelation's overall capacity to equip an ancient audience to embrace its distinctive Christian identity in their current circumstances. Revelation has continued to inform Christian self-understanding in subsequent centuries, as well. Learning to read Revelation well, according to what kind of literature it is, is an essential piece of engaging the book's ideas faithfully and intelligently.

Probably no New Testament writing is as regularly misunderstood as Revelation. It strikes modern audiences as bizarre because they lack familiarity with its literary form and theological rhetoric. Revelation is, as the opening word in the book's original Greek version indicates, an "apocalypse" (*apokalupsis*). As a "revelation," it is an unveiling; it purports to be the record of visions experienced by a believer named John. Those visions, John reports, were given by God to show Christ-followers in a Roman setting "what must soon take place" (Rev 1:1). With the book's description of a witness receiving privileged insights into heavenly activity, a heavy dose of symbolism, visions of grotesque beasts as obvious representations of a rapacious empire and its self-conceit, a thoroughly dualistic outlook about cosmic struggles that define reality, a deterministic theology in which God exercises supreme control, and depictions of God waging battle against spiritual adversaries, Revelation takes its place alongside other apocalypses that were produced by Jewish authors (e.g., Dan 7–12; 4 Ezra) and later by Christian authors (e.g., Shepherd of Hermas, Apocalypse of Peter). Revelation is the only full-fledged Christian "apocalypse" that found itself included in the New Testament (cf. Mark 13 and parallels).

Throughout history Revelation has attracted significant disgust from some Christian readers. Others have found themselves inordinately fascinated by the book. Revelation's strangeness fuels both kinds of reactions. Disgust arises from what appears to be an especially vindictive streak in the book's perspective on divine judgment and a nearly unmitigated misogynistic outlook on female characters and symbolism. On the other hand, fascination stirs readers who presume that clues to specific future events lie hidden in Revelation. The purpose of Revelation, however, appears to direct attention elsewhere. At its heart the book delivers an uncompromising denunciation of idolatry and an earnest appeal for unswerving devotion to Christ. Revelation exhorts its audience to bear witness to Christ, to offer a lived expression of singular faithfulness to him. Such fidelity requires believers to keep themselves unstained by adversarial spiritual forces and separate from an imperial system whose self-regard and social conventions demand a blasphemous loyalty from those who dwell within the empire's borders. Among its original audience, the book implored Christ-followers to resist the Roman Empire's corruptive influences. How or why Revelation might encourage modern Christ-followers to adopt similarly uncompromising postures is a topic that frequently generates lively debates.

The Book's Origins and Ancient Audience

A man named John takes credit for writing Revelation, claiming that he did so as a response to a command from Jesus himself (Rev 1:1–2, 9–20; 22:8). John identifies himself as God's "slave" (although the NRSV offers a tamer translation of "servant" in Rev 1:1) and a fellow Christian "brother" (Rev 1:9). He refers briefly to "the persecution" or oppression he has endured and to the location of his visionary experiences on the small island of Patmos in the Aegean Sea, not far from the western coast of modern Turkey (Rev 1:9–10). If John had been punished for identifying as a Christ-follower, possibly he had to flee to Patmos or had been exiled there, although there is no way to know for sure. He might have been merely engaged in ministry on the island, and the hardship he notes might have been ostracism and not a more grievous form of harassment.

Because Revelation was likely composed near the close of the first century, and because of a brief reference to the twelve apostles as foundational figures with a lasting but completed legacy (Rev 21:14), the John who wrote Revelation could not have been the same John who was one of Jesus' twelve original apostles. Differences in literary style and theological emphasis make it clear that this John did not write either the Gospel with that name or the Johannine Letters, either. The name *John* was common among Jews in the Roman era, and so all that remains known about the author of Revelation is what he divulges in the book itself. His identity remains as mysterious as some of the images and scenes in the book he wrote.

The book never explicitly quotes a piece of the Jewish Scriptures, but it makes countless allusions to scriptural texts. Scores of familiar scriptural images, such as the tree of life (Rev 2:7, 22:2; Gen 2:9; 3:22–24), words like a sharp sword (Rev 1:16; 2:12, 16; 19:15, 21; Isa 49:2), a divine throne with all the colors of a rainbow (Rev 4:3; Ezek 1:26–28), horrific plagues (Rev 15–16; Exod 7:14–12:32), and a sweet-tasting scroll (Rev 10:9–10; Ezek 3:1–3) give Revelation's rhetoric a sense of scriptural emulation richer than any other New Testament writing's. Whoever John was, he knew Judaism's most prized texts well. The book's rich scriptural fluency also gives the revelatory rhetoric a kind of trustworthy familiarity. Revelation does not make its case by drawing on an author's authority; it does so by making connections with Scripture. Weaving in allusions to so many texts and images, the book speaks with a familiar voice.

Revelation's syntax also evidently speaks in a particular tone to the book's audience. The syntax distinguishes itself by blending conventional Greek patterns with Semitic ones. That tendency might reveal something about the author: that his native language was not Greek or that he deliberately tried to emphasize a different kind of ethnic identity over against the eastern Roman Empire's standard lingua franca. In any case, the end result—how the syntax propels the book's rhetoric—is more important and more easily analyzed than John's cultural background. By presenting its visions in a voice that reflects multiple cultures, refusing to let Greek speak alone without any Hebrew undertones, Revelation teaches with a rhetoric that itself refuses to assimilate to conventional standards. The book speaks as if it is a cultural outsider or an immigrant who makes no apologies for and even defiantly revels in speaking another's language with a pronounced foreign accent.

John apparently knew the audiences that Revelation addresses. The book presents itself to seven churches in the Roman province of Asia, which corresponds to the western part of modern Turkey. All of those churches were located in prominent cities, and all of those cities were relatively cosmopolitan and religiously diverse. Most notable, during the first century CE all seven of the cities actively participated in the imperial cult, hosting ceremonies or civic events that honored Roman emperors as divine beings. The anti-imperial rhetoric of Revelation likely made an acute and sobering impression on those particular audiences.

Revelation's second and third chapters deliver specific messages to the seven churches. Claiming to do so at Jesus' behest, John transcribed a unique message for each church. All seven messages are brief but not to the extent of being generic. John knew specific details about those communities, it seems, including their difficulties, their shortcomings, and the internal divisions that afflicted them. He addresses them in various ways, as one committed to their well-being, for he encourages some and reproves others. Urgency saturates his counsel. He views the hazards that potentially confront believers as fierce and the need for churches' faithful endurance as indispensable. Repeatedly, the messages speak of rewards for believers who "conquer." John addresses the churches as an authoritative figure, with a confidence and clout fueled by the visions he has seen and the instructions he has heard. Revelation is therefore not an attempt to document visions or predictions for their own sake; the book is largely about exhortation. It calls its audiences to persevere in the midst of peril, motivating them with a vision of a faithful and powerful God who sees their struggles and is determined to rescue them in the end from godless oppressors that torment them.

Revelation's specific origins remain difficult to determine. It is not clear exactly when John wrote this document, for it makes no entirely unambiguous references to specific historical events. Rather conspicuous allusions to the destruction of the Jerusalem temple and the tyranny of Emperor Nero indicate a date after 70 CE, however. Anytime between 70 and 95 is possible, with very old Christian traditions locating the book's origins in the 90s, during the final years of Emperor Domitian's reign, which ended with his assassination in 96. Some interpreters speculate that Revelation may have been composed over time in stages, but those hypotheses do not necessarily have a great impact on how one might begin to interpret this intriguing book.

According to Revelation 2–3, the Christian communities in Asia were hardly all alike during the end of the first century. Not all of them appear to have been suffering harassment or the threat of hopelessness, even though John refers to a common "persecution" (Rev 1:9). The church in Laodicea, for example, enjoyed prosperity and relative comfort (Rev 3:17). The Laodiceans' problem was an inflated sense of security and confidence. The churches in Smyrna and Philadelphia were evidently enduring friction with local Jews, but it is not clear whether those churches themselves were composed of Jewish believers, gentile believers, or a mix of both (Rev 2:9, 3:9). Several of the communities were suffering strife because they were contaminated, from John's perspective, by the presence of false teachings and false prophets (Rev 2:14–15, 20, 24).

The messages to the seven churches do include a couple of references to hostilities and physical threats: an otherwise unknown man named Antipas had been killed in Pergamum (Rev 2:13), and the believers in Smyrna evidently feared imprisonment and possible death (Rev 2:10). Those passages appear to refer to sporadic and isolated outbursts against members of churches. No other sources give solid evidence of systematic persecution of Christ-followers in Asia during the first century. It is therefore likely that the book's additional references to violent and widespread persecution (e.g., Rev 6:9–11; 17:6; 20:4) either represent well-known atrocities in the past, such as Nero's persecution of believers in Rome during the mid-60s CE, or describe what the author anticipates will happen "soon" as conflicts intensify over time (e.g., Rev 1:1, 22:6). Indeed, the book views collisions between churches and imperial forces as inevitable once believers bear witness to Christ with the intensity the author desires. To be a faithful witness, according to Revelation, means giving full allegiance to Christ, which will certainly incur the Roman Empire's wrath and thus further expose its abuses and godlessness.

If there is a central or dominant theological message that propels Revelation in all of its visionary disclosures, teachings, and warnings, it is this: Jesus Christ is Lord over all. The book articulates that message over and over to advance a particular purpose: to motivate the audience to take actions that appropriately reflect Christ's majesty. Revelation, like most apocalyptic literature of its time, aimed to buttress an audience's confidence in God by disclosing the veiled ways in which God is actively engaged in combating evil. The book also exhorts its readers to withhold their fealty from the Roman Empire and the empire's blasphemous pretense. In some of its most haunting images, Revelation offers a scathing denunciation of the Roman Empire, especially by laying bare the obscene excesses in the empire's attempts to maintain its cultural and commercial supremacy. John wanted his audience to be aware of the truth about Rome and to position themselves as distinctive *from* the empire. He also warns his readers about the destruction that false teachers can cause. He desperately wanted to see the Christian communities of his time and place be alert and shun complacency.

In sum, Revelation urges the seven churches and, by extension, all churches to embrace their primary identity and calling as communities that bear witness to Christ even when they find themselves surrounded by contrary values or outright wickedness. They should proclaim Christ as Lord even as they draw confidence from that truth to know that God is present among them and one day will intervene in human history to bring about a new, transformed existence. Churches that bear authentic witness about Christ may actually spark opposition and resentment in such a volatile setting, but such are the hazards of testifying about a Lord who promises an alternative society and challenges the regnant systems of perpetual greed, evil, idolatry, and injustice.

Overview

Introduction (Rev 1)

Immediately at the beginning, Revelation states some of its key focal points. The book is a "prophecy" (Rev 1:3; cf. 22:7, 10, 18–19; 19:10), telling truths that must be heeded. It speaks about what must happen "soon" (Rev 1:1; cf. 22:6, 7, 12, 20) and notes the urgency of its message because "the time is near" (Rev 1:3; cf. 22:10). The frame created by terms and themes that appear in both the opening and the concluding chapters adds emphasis to the author's attempts to rouse his audience into action and wakefulness, especially when that language directs focus toward developments that are about to occur.

The book's initial references to Jesus Christ are majestic. He is "the firstborn of the dead" and also "the ruler of the kings of the earth" (Rev 1:5; cf. Col 1:18). His highly symbolic and awe-inspiring appearance makes John fall to the ground in fear. The risen Christ is no mere mortal, for John's description emphasizes purity, strength, and mastery. Christ declares he now possesses power over death itself and Hades. At first Revelation refers to the risen Christ as distinct from God, who occupies a throne. But the image of a radiant Christ nevertheless evokes other writings' descriptions of God (e.g., Ezek 1:26–28, Dan 10:5–9). Distinctions between Jesus and God occasionally blur as Revelation proceeds. For example, at the beginning of the book, "the Lord God" is "the Alpha and the Omega" (Rev 1:8), the sum of all things; at the end of Revelation, Jesus makes the same claim about himself (Rev 22:13; cf. 21:6, 22).

Seven Messages to Seven Churches (Rev 2–3)

Revelation emphasizes Jesus' presence among the churches to which John writes: Jesus walks among the lampstands that represent the seven communities and holds the stars that symbolize the angels assigned to each church. The book further accents Christ's ongoing involvement with those Christ-followers when each message to a given church includes Christ saying "I know" particular details of that church's common life.

While each of the seven communiques has its own particular message, all of them adhere to a recognizable form. They begin by attributing their content to Jesus, using language consistent with John's description of him in Revelation 1. After each "I know" statement, Jesus offers an analysis of a given church's situation. Attention is given to the "works" of most of the seven churches (cf. Rev 18:6; 20:12–13; 22:12). Except for the analyses of Smyrna and Philadelphia, Jesus criticizes aspects of each community. Instructions and commands play a part in all of the analyses. Each church also receives some kind of a promise about what Jesus will do for those people who "conquer" (cf. Rev 21:7).

The messages to the churches never flesh out all of the details of what it might look like to "conquer," but the book generally equates conquering with a faithfulness to God that remains resolute, even if it leads to death. Jesus' words to believers in Smyrna suggest as much, for he asserts that life awaits those who are "faithful until death" and "whoever conquers" (Rev 2:10–11). Later in Revelation, a heavenly elder tells John that Jesus Christ "has conquered," yet the surrounding context describes this victorious Christ as a slaughtered lamb (Rev 5:5–6). Jesus thus provides the prime example of the specific kind of conquering to which Revelation calls the churches. Jesus is "the faithful witness" who died (Rev 1:5; cf. 3:14). He is, in an ironic image, a slaughtered conqueror.

Antipas of Pergamum, when he was killed, followed in Christ's footsteps as a "witness" and "faithful one" (Rev 2:13). The Greek word for "witness," *martus*, resides behind the English word *martyr*, a person whose stubborn refusal to renounce a devotion or testimony results in death. Revelation can claim some responsibility for the convention of defining "martyrdom" as the killing of a person because of their religious devotion. As Revelation sees it, those witnesses who die as a result of giving testimony about Christ actually bear witness again—and perhaps more fully—in their deaths, for they die as Jesus did, innocently and at the hands of opponents (cf. Rev 6:9–10; 7:13–17; 17:6). This way of celebrating Jesus' and some of his followers' deaths, as demonstrations of their unwavering commitment to God, became quite influential in Christian thought later in the history of the early church.

The kind of living "witness" that Revelation commends is a life of exclusive devotion to Christ. The author's interrelated rhetoric about conquering, testimony, witnesses, unflinching allegiance, opposition, and death therefore imagines extremely high stakes for Christ-followers who live as the book expects. Ostracism or worse might have been possible results, especially for the book's original audiences, who lived in settings where public religious devotion to the Roman emperor was common and perhaps expected.

As mentioned, the messages to the various communities in Asia do not indicate that all of the churches were facing persecution when John wrote. Perhaps, as Revelation sees it, the absence of persecution was an aberration that could not last much longer if churches started to bear witness in the more vigorous and defiant ways the book advocates. Perhaps the relative calm among the churches in Asia exposed indifference and a lack of passion within the churches themselves, as if John aimed to criticize them for being eager to remain assimilated within their wider society and its value systems. In any case, the book calls the seven communities to a different existence, urging them to understand their identity and roles as witnesses, specifically witnesses in the mold of Christ himself. Not only was Christ the one who was faithful to God and God's intentions, up to the point of suffering rejection and death, but he also was the one whose witness and sufferings exposed the violence of evil—an evil manifested through a society's determination to promote its own ends and its own dominance. Revelation's seven messages to the churches therefore refuse to let Christ-followers think they can remain spiritually languid and take the dangers of idolatry and falsehood lightly (e.g., Rev 2:7, 14–15, 20–24; 3:9). Those believers need to see the truth behind those illusions, and so Revelation turns to disclose hidden things to them.

A Scroll Sealed with Seven Seals, Opened by the Lamb (Rev 4:1–8:1)

When Jesus' trumpetlike voice summons John through a door to heaven, the book's scope of vision expands greatly. John enters a throne room where angelic beings sing praise to God, who sits on the throne. Their songs evoke the words of the seraphim's cries when God appeared to the prophet Isaiah (Isa 6:3). God's holiness and majesty elicit worship.

God produces a scroll that has been secured with seven seals, and only Jesus Christ is deemed worthy to break open the seals and therefore to bring to light what God has authorized. Revelation implies that only Jesus, because he has "conquered," holds the key to bringing God's intentions or plan to pass. Jesus has unleashed the new realities to come because of his victory through death.

This part of Revelation does not identify Jesus by name but as "a Lamb standing as if it had been slaughtered" (Rev 5:6). This same "Lamb" is also "the Lion of the tribe of Judah, the Root of David" (Rev 5:5; cf. Gen 49:8–10; Isa 11:10). Nevertheless, the image of a lamb that is both vulnerable (always somehow visibly manifesting the reality of its slaughter) and powerful (having seven horns and seven eyes) gets all the attention when those in the throne room burst into song. The angelic beings ascribe "blessing and honor and glory and might" to both the Lamb and "the one seated on the throne," blurring the distinction between Jesus Christ and God (Rev 5:13).

When the praise subsides and the Lamb opens the seven seals, each of the first six triggers world-altering events. A conquering king goes forth to battle. The people of the world turn on one another in lethal violence. Food shortages and price gouging occur. The natural world shows its deadly force through famine, disease, and wild beasts. Martyrs—literally people who bear witness or provide testimony, those who "had been slaughtered for the word of God and [their] testimony" (Rev 6:9)—reveal themselves and cry impatiently for justice. Earthquakes strike, and the heavens fall apart. When the Lamb breaks the seventh seal, there is silence.

The upheavals that flow from the gradual opening of the scroll have a sense of comprehensive devastation; nearly everything about existence in the world appears dangerous or targeted for destruction. The cumulative sense is one of humanity's habitat suffering a nearly absolute collapse, although some of this is through what appear to be the ordinary activities of human beings and not always so-called natural causes or natural disasters. At the same time as all the widespread loss occurs, John speaks about angels protecting the earth, the sea, and the trees; the earth's riches have value and are worth defending. John also sees a huge multitude of people from all of Israel's twelve tribes. Those 144,000 people "[came] out of the great ordeal" and wear white robes, symbolizing the purity they received from "the blood of the Lamb" (Rev 7:14). God and the Lamb give them shelter, nourishment, relief, and solace. As things fall apart, still God proves faithful to God's people.

Seven Trumpets of Judgment (Rev 8:2–11:19)

More widespread destruction occurs when seven angels each blow a trumpet. The book describes awful results, including hail, fire, celestial transformations, a darkened atmosphere, an invasion of fierce locusts, death, and plagues. Huge numbers of people die. Ships are destroyed, disabling maritime trade. The earth suffers ecological devastation with destroyed forests and grasslands, poisoned seas, and acrid air. The damage is not entirely indiscriminate, however, for those who bear "the seal of God" enjoy some protection amid the chaos. Moreover, the final trumpet turns the focus away from ruin and toward newness. The seventh trumpet announces the arrival of God's reign in all of its fullness, promising a new and eternal era in which God will rule. The trumpets thus point forward toward the eventual transformation of all things.

The calamities unleashed after trumpet peals appear to have a purpose, or at least they provide a particular opportunity: to urge people to repent. The cataclysms suggest a progression toward the time at which God will finally prove to be Lord over the world, a world currently marked by violence, persecution, and idolatry perpetrated by those who need to repent—those who refuse to "give up worshiping demons and idols of gold and silver and bronze and stone and wood, which cannot see or hear or walk" (Rev 9:20–21). The distresses the world suffers provide signs of an approaching end. They are frightful harbingers of God's judgment. It remains unclear from John's descriptions, however, that the portents and destructions can succeed at prompting anyone to repent.

At the same time, the signs of the world's anguish are general in their description. The consequences of the seven trumpets resemble many of the consequences of the seven seals. Later in the book, seven bowls of wrath will recall those consequences. The generalized character of the imagery and the magnitude of the destructions make for poetic and evocative rhetoric, not encryption of precise events. Revelation does not describe a strict sequential progression through specifically identifiable disasters, wars, and outbreaks. Rather, the book speaks of patterns and recurrences that occur as God's intentions move toward their sevenfold fulfillment. The book's fascination with the number seven, representing divine perfection, offers a symbolic statement about the completion and wholeness of God's plan. The plan must play itself out to its full goal, but the route to that goal will remain almost repetitive, as if the world is stuck in its destructive tendencies and creation is somehow ordained to experience ongoing upheavals. The road to eventual fulfillment remains persistently marked, over and over again, by distress in the world, by severe admonitions for idolaters and evildoers to repent, and by resolute hope for the ultimate realization of God's reign.

Even with the generalized imagery, Revelation's visions include details that the book's original audience would have connected to familiar events and people. When John measures the temple, as a prophet before him once did (Ezek 40–42), he makes a statement that God knows and preserves the Jerusalem temple and its contours, as well as the people who worship there. In an enigmatic statement about "the nations" (gentiles) who are allowed to "trample" on the temple and Jerusalem for a designated period (Rev 11:2; cf. Luke 21:24), believers at the end of the first century CE would have recognized a rather obvious allusion to the end of the Great Revolt. Even with the holy building's recent demolition, however, Revelation asserts that God has held on to the true temple and those who belong there (cf. Rev 11:19, 21:22), just as God did during Ezekiel's day, during the Babylonian exile. With that reference to the recent tragedy in Jerusalem, Revelation therefore does something other than speak of struggles that stand in some far-off future. The book tells its original audience, instead, that they are already in the midst of world-altering trials. The time of transformation has already begun. The time of completion, when God and the Messiah will reign in a renewed creation, is already on its way.

Battles against Satan (the Dragon) and the Beasts (Rev 12–14)

John's visions expand in this section, for he sees an even wider range of otherworldly realities. The portents tell of a cosmic battle with the appearance of "a woman clothed with the sun" and "a great red dragon, with seven heads and ten horns" (Rev 12:1, 3). John never identifies the woman, but he names the dragon as "the Devil and Satan" (Rev 12:9; cf. 20:2). The heavenly woman does not necessarily have to represent a single being or thing. In any case, her specific identity is less important in the vision than her function as a mother who is kept secure while she brings others into existence. In an apparent reference to Christ, she bears a son who goes to God's throne before the dragon can devour him. In an apparent reference to believers, she also bears children "who keep the commandments of God and hold the testimony of Jesus" (Rev 12:17). The dragon, whom God's angels cast down to earth, makes war against those children. By emphasizing the woman's successful protection and the value of her children, the vision declares God's supremacy over Satan. In addition, the vision identifies Satan as the chief adversary of the people of God while it also celebrates a creative and fertile power at the heart of God's activity in the midst of an otherwise destructive cosmic conflict.

Two powerful beasts emerge in Revelation 13, one from the sea and one out of the earth. Both of them operate according to the dragon's authority, serving his purposes. The beasts rule the world, perpetuate lies, promote blasphemy, brand people like they are slaves, persecute their enemies, and receive both worship and adulation from the earth's population. The characterization of the beasts calls attention to the abuses of imperial power and unmasks that power as satanic in origin. Specific features of the beasts recall Daniel's vision of the ancient Near East's great empires through history (Dan 7). Like the empires that historically harassed Israel and Judah, the beasts promote idolatry even as they dominate the nations militarily and economically.

The beasts also appear to recall the Roman Empire in particular, insofar as one has seven heads, which correspond to the seven hills on which Rome was built (cf. Rev 17:7–14). In addition, the number 666 and the references to a healed "mortal wound" (Rev 13:3, 12, 18) likely evoke associations with Nero, whose rule was distinguished by his fanatical madness and persecution of Christ-followers. When "Nero Caesar" is written in Hebrew, the numerical equivalents of the Hebrew letters total 666. Moreover, concerning the healed wound, in the late first century, rumors circulated that Nero had actually survived his suicide attempt in 68 CE and was hiding in the Roman East until a time when he would reappear on the public stage. Some people even thought Nero would be reborn in some capacity. Revelation sees the spirit of Nero's prideful lunacy woven throughout the empire's abuses. His abominations were hardly aberrations of the empire's values; his legacy therefore extended into John's setting. Nero was dead at the end of the first century, but Revelation insinuates to its audience that the chaos and abuse for which he was renowned are surely coming back.

In contrast to the dragon and the pair of terrible beasts stands the Lamb, elevated on Mount Zion. A blameless multitude resides securely with the Lamb; they are marked on their foreheads with his name and the name of his Father, the true God. Exacerbating and finalizing the sense of a clear division between the Lamb's society and the beast's society, a harvest occurs, representing a final judgment in which those loyal to the beast must endure God's wrath. Judgment happens worldwide, and the imagery is gruesome: "the great wine press of the wrath of God" produces a flood of blood squeezed from "the vintage of the earth" (Rev 14:19–20). If anyone laments the vast carnage, John makes no mention of it.

Plagues from Seven Bowls and the Destruction of Babylon (Rev 15:1–19:10)

The next "portent" John recounts is another series of calamitous events. Some of them resonate with the sevenfold effects of the previously described seals and the trumpets, further suggesting that Revelation offers a kaleidoscopic collection of prophecies and not a linear timetable of discrete future events. When angels pour out sundry plagues from bowls, almost every aspect of the earth's geography suffers a form of destruction, and the planet's residents suffer greatly. It appears as though everything that makes the created world distinctive or safe becomes unmade.

John then follows an angel to witness the destruction of Babylon, which was foretold earlier in the book (Rev 14:8). The ancient Mesopotamian city of Babylon, once the site of imperial majesty, obviously predated Revelation by centuries, and Revelation offers strong hints to indicate that it uses "Babylon" as a cipher for something else (cf. 1 Pet 5:13). The book is not alone in doing so: after Roman troops looted and burned the Jerusalem temple in 70 CE, Jewish authors began to use the name of the infamous city to refer to Rome. In addition, the imagery Revelation uses to describe Babylon's power and wealth aptly characterizes Rome. The point of narrating Babylon's downfall, and doing so with both disgust and glee, is to demonstrate God's supremacy over any empire and any imperial idolatry. From John's point of view, Rome was simply the current and most familiar iteration of an imperial system that openly defies God, God's expectations for justice, and the well-being of God's people.

A "great whore" (Rev 17:1) serves as a rather unsubtle personification of Babylon and of imperial atrocities in general (cf. other prostitute-like cities in Isa 23:17 and Nah 3:4). Clothed in opulence, she gets drunk on "the blood of the witnesses to Jesus." Like the city of Rome itself, she sits on seven hills. She holds authority over many "nations and languages." As a prostitute, she takes "the kings of the earth" to bed with her, suggesting Rome's power over others, Rome's ability to seduce the world through its pleasures and wealth, and other rulers' willingness to ally with Rome for their mutual benefit. Those who willingly partner with Rome or submit to the empire's beguilement have aligned themselves with the blasphemous nature of Revelation's prostitute, as signified by the hideous scarlet beast she rides. It bears notice that the persistent sexual imagery used to describe Babylon becomes problematic for several reasons. For one thing, Revelation views this particular prostitute as the source and never the victim of sexual and economic exploitation. She therefore represents a flawed yet familiar stereotype about prostitution that Revelation tacitly endorses. In addition, repeated references to corrupting and intoxicating "fornication" (e.g., Rev 14:8; 17:2, 4; 18:3, 9; 19:2) with Rome refer less to actual sexual activity that offends John and more to a representation of idolatry that defiles all who participate in it. Revelation is quick to characterize defilement and false worship with sexual terminology.

Despite its power, Babylon proves no equal to God. The announcement of God's judgment on the imperious city prompts a series of responses, magnifying the pathos and also extending a sense of delight in the city's fall (cf. Jer 50–51). In one response, angelic voices speak of the empire's atrocities, and they beseech God's people to disavow any association with Babylon: "Come out of her . . . so that you do not take part in her sins" (Rev 18:4). Babylon's imperial allies, depicted as her idolatrous sexual partners, respond by lamenting her loss. Merchants weep and wail because without her no one remains to purchase luxury goods at lucrative prices. Those who mourn her downfall are the powerful and the wealthy. All the inhabitants of heaven, however, offer full-throated praise to God and anticipate the coming marriage of the Lamb and his bride. This bride will turn out to be a new city in which God's people dwell eternally and safely with God (Rev 21:2, 9–10).

Final Victories and the Arrival of a New Society (Rev 19:11–22:21)

When Christ rides forth from heaven, in a vision of his grand reappearance (cf. Rev 16:14–15; 22:20; Matt 24:42–44; 1 Thess 5:2; 2 Pet 3:10), followed by "the armies of heaven," he resembles a warrior, not a lamb (Rev 19:11–16). Apparently the ferocity of the enemies to be annihilated requires a serious display of divine strength to defeat them; a slaughtered lamb alone cannot complete the task. Although "the beast and the kings of the earth with their armies" (Rev 19:19) oppose Christ, the battle John recounts appears easily won. Birds feast on the flesh of the dead, while the beast and a false prophet (cf. Rev 16:13) are cast into "the lake of fire," with no one in Revelation expressing compassion or horror in response to the punishments.

In a series of tantalizingly brief descriptions of monumental events in Rev 20:1–10, an angel banishes Satan to a bottomless pit for a thousand years, slaughtered martyrs reign with Christ for that same duration, and then after that period Satan enjoys one final opportunity to deceive the nations before he is cast forever into the lake of fire and sulfur. Revelation acknowledges it will be a battle, but the book expresses no doubt that God will finally defeat the source of evil and godlessness. Finally, judgment occurs before the throne of God. Even Death and Hades, personified as actual beings, lose their power over people they once held in their grip and suffer eternal destruction. For everyone whose name appears in "the book of life," no more opponents or oppressors remain. The cosmic strife comes at last to an end.

A new society then begins. Themes of divine presence and human flourishing infuse the book's descriptions of "a new heaven and a new earth" (Rev 21:1; cf. Isa 65:17). Even though Revelation names those two places separately at first, John's vision of the future maintains no clear distinction between the pair. A new dwelling, "the new Jerusalem," comes out of heaven and God dwells in this city, along with mortals. Believers are not taken away from the earth to dwell with God in a far-off heaven. It is as if old understandings of heaven and earth merge in a single, terrestrial setting.

Although ancient Rome considered itself "the Eternal City," Revelation associates God's new society with a different city. Yet this is not the same old Jerusalem with a fresh coat of paint. John's description calls attention to several transformations. A physical temple no longer is necessary, for "the Lord God the Almighty and the Lamb" themselves *are* the temple (Rev 21:22). No sun or moon illuminates this place, for God and the Lamb provide light. The stuff of which the massive city is made, fine metals and gems, radiates a sense of purity and perfection. Absent from the new dwelling are things that once afflicted humankind: death, mourning, idolatry, and moral pollution (cf. Isa 25:8). There is no sea there, either, probably because in Jewish cosmology the watery depths represented the forces of chaos.

The physical description of the walled and radiant city may have an antiseptic feel about it until one notices that the new Jerusalem also houses a thriving and open society. "The nations" dwell in this city and circulate within it, for its gates are never closed (in contrast to the temple gate in Ezek 44:1–3). The nations' honor and glory stream into the city and enrich it (cf. Isa 60:11). There is no sense of exploitation, as there was in so many of Revelation's earlier visions. The book imagines a culture that enjoys plenty and fullness without obtaining those blessings through the mistreatment of certain segments of society. The city openly welcomes inhabitants into its limits. When Revelation gets to its final sentences, the book invites its audience to take part in the glorious future God will create, exhorting them to "come" and receive the benefits of the new Jerusalem "as a gift."

The arrival of a new society also means the arrival of a new ecosystem with thriving vegetation and fresh water. Revelation's depictions of wrathful devastation have often been taken to promote a view of the earth as a doomed world, a planet destined for extinction and therefore not worth stewarding. But the book's ending turns the focus from destruction to restoration. At one point Revelation voices criticism of "those who destroy the earth" (Rev 11:18), and the description of the new Jerusalem in Revelation 21–22 similarly expresses God's desire to provide blessings through natural elements. A river runs through the city (cf. Ezek 47:1–12), providing sustenance from "the throne of God and of the Lamb" to whoever wants it, as "a gift." The tree of life provides nourishment and healing for everyone, with no permanent divisions established by cultural or ethnic criteria. The city remains a sure refuge from the defilements that characterized life with the dragon, beasts, and Babylon. As a place that ensures a life of purity, plenty, fecundity, and intimacy with God, the new Jerusalem intimates the restoration of Eden, although now in an urbanized landscape (cf. Gen 2:8–16). The New Testament's final depictions of what God intends for human existence share much in common with the Old Testament's first depictions.

The Book's Themes and Theological Emphases

Worship, Praise, and the Ends of God

No other New Testament book is as full of song as Revelation. John describes heavenly beings who sing praise to God, some of them "without ceasing" (Rev 4:8). The lyrical praise extols God's holiness, glory, and faithfulness (e.g., Rev 4:8, 11; 5:13; 11:16–18; 15:3–4) and also Christ the Lamb's power and blessing (e.g., Rev 5:9–13). In many instances, even though the book does not refer explicitly to singing, figures whom John sees in his visions erupt in loud praise that reasserts God's might (e.g., Rev 11:15; 12:10–12; 16:5–7; 19:1–8; 21:3–4). As a result of its hymnic prose, as well as that prose's ability to provide new expressions of familiar scriptural claims and images, Revelation has inspired countless songs and liturgies for Christian worship.

Revelation's songs and theological declarations are as doxological as the book's visions can be frightening. The frequent expressions of praise play an important role in the book's copious visions of devastation, war, and judgment. The praise offers regular reminders that the world and its fate are not progressing through time in an arbitrary or meaningless way. Whatever may come, the book insists, God can be trusted to bring about a just and holy outcome to the travails of life. That is because the frequent expressions of praise refuse to see the events of Revelation as random or casually considered. The fate of creation, its inhabitants, and even powerful cosmic beings rests in God's control.

Exuberant claims about God's sovereignty or divine determinism have created problems for Christian theology, especially in recent centuries, because of ethical and scientific objections to the belief that

God exercises authority over events and human choices. Nevertheless, a belief in God as the Lord over history, as the one who determines the fates of nations, was a theological staple of ancient apocalyptic literature, just as the New Testament frequently makes similar assertions (e.g., Dan 2:21a, 4:17; Acts 4:24–28; Rom 13:1–4). Revelation's doxological rhetoric does not necessarily describe God as a puppeteer of minutiae, controlling every historical development, however. The book keeps its primary focus on the end of things—what God will accomplish in an ultimate struggle to defeat evil and establish holiness and newness. Only God can bring things to a desirable conclusion, and therefore only God deserves praise (cf. Rev 22:8–9). The book is less interested in trying to assert that God holds sway over every earthquake, outbreak of disease, or solar eclipse.

The praise in Revelation therefore contributes to the book's ability to express a willing and almost desperate embrace of God's power and goodness, as if God's ability to reign and to establish a secure existence for people remains humanity's and all creation's only hope. If God's ultimate aim in establishing a divine rule over all creation was anything other than to extend holiness, security, and abundance, then the book's statements of praise should appear to audiences as just as terrifying as its descriptions of plagues. If the Almighty God, as Revelation depicts the Divine, were not determined to be "among mortals" and to "wipe every tear from their eyes" (Rev 21:3–4), then Revelation might give its readers little reason to face the future with an eager hope. The book would likewise lack a compelling justification for why believers should bear witness for Christ. Praise provides reassurance to an audience only if the claims embedded in the praise align with a reassuring portrait of God and God's goals. In other words, praise would be deadly if God were just like the dragon and if God's power functioned in the same way. Revelation insists that praise directed toward an all-powerful and just God is utterly well-founded, at least for those who find themselves preserved from God's wrath and sheltered from God's enemies.

The Roman Empire, and Empires in General

No other New Testament book is as acidly critical of the Roman Empire as Revelation. With its description of the beasts who are agents of Satan the dragon and its unflattering portrait of Babylon "the great whore," Revelation offers a vastly different perspective than other New

Testament authors who commend a more conciliatory posture toward Roman rule (e.g., Rom 13:1–4; 1 Tim 2:1–2; 1 Pet 2:17). Those writers do not see the insidious heart of an empire, at least not with the same eyes and sense of exigency that Revelation possesses. John's visions characterize imperial pretensions as blasphemous and idolatrous and therefore a source of defilement. Just as Jeremiah spoke of ancient Babylon sinking like a stone in a river (Jer 51:63–64), Revelation yearns for all that Babylon symbolizes to suffer the same demise (Rev 18:21). The book sees empire as rotten to the core. There appear to be many reasons why John's visions take such a negative view of Rome in particular and empire in general.

One reason for Revelation's criticism of empire resides in frequent references to intoxication and "fornication" (e.g., Rev 2:14, 20–22; 9:21; 14:8; 17:2, 4; 18:3, 9; 19:2). Those images note the allure of Rome and also the way in which an empire works through forming wide-reaching alliances that provide mutual benefit, especially to those who enjoy privileges reserved for the ruling classes. As mentioned already, occasional connections between fornication and idolatry (e.g., Rev 2:14, 20–22; 21:8; 22:15) also suggest that Rome provides a fertile sociopolitical soil for idolatrous presumptions and activities. The depiction of Babylon focuses on outspoken abominations and blasphemies, which could refer in part to the elevated claims that Rome—like any other empire—made about itself.

But there is also more to the picture of Revelation's concerns about an empire's perils. An imperial network of idolatry extends beyond an empire's prideful attitude or the excesses of patriotism. Revelation sees idolatry embedded in the reality of what was required for ancient people to do business with Rome and to navigate the Roman social world without arousing suspicion or suffering economic backlash. If indeed participation in the imperial cult, in which deceased and living emperors were honored as divinities, was essentially expected and not optional in the province of Asia, then Christ-followers there were faced with the prospect of committing idolatry on a regular basis, just to navigate their ordinary existence. Revelation tells its audience that they cannot be loyal—or "faithful"—to both Christ and this religiously promiscuous empire. At the same time, the book is not very clear about exactly what kinds of activities would constitute an unacceptable display of loyalty to Rome. The theological rhetoric would seem to rule out emperor worship and probably also participation in certain exploitative economic practices. But John appears so zealous in the messages to the seven churches that it is possible his scorn might also have extended even to lower-key social activities such as sharing meals with unbelievers and participating in local trade guilds. The Roman system's capacity for defilement was, according to Revelation, almost absolute and hardly limited to temples and formal ceremonies.

Revelation also criticizes the ways in which the imperial mechanism treats its subjects like slaves. Occasional mention of people who bear the empire's mark (e.g., Rev 13:16–17, 14:9–11, 16:1–2) brings to mind the practice of branding one's own slaves. God's people also bear marks, but they do so as God's slaves (Rev 7:2–3; 9:4). The empire, however, treats its people as expendable possessions. It demands acquiescence, allowing no one to opt out of complying with its systems and expectations. Out of Satanic impulses, the empire even chooses to "make war" on the people who refuse to express their fealty to it and its values (e.g., Rev 11:7, 12:17, 13:7). This empire consumes its own subjects to sustain itself. John hints also about a self-destructive aspect lodged in the empire's dehumanizing ethos, both in noting how the empire exploits its people and also in a strange, unexplained comment: many peoples and even the beast "will hate the whore" of Babylon (Rome) and eventually devour her (Rev 17:16). The empire's own consumptive and domineering tendencies will contribute to its eventual destruction. Rome feeds the beast's appetite, and the beast will outlive it. Rome was neither the first nor the last of the world's great empires. Just as Rome looked to John as Babylon once looked to John's spiritual ancestors, perhaps the book implies that other empires could come along later, bearing a striking resemblance to Rome and allied with the same vicious beast. It is not difficult to guess how John might have evaluated them.

Revelation's criticism of empire also has economic dimensions. Personified Babylon's general disregard for its subjects, combined with its immoral addiction to wealth, drives it to desire more for its most powerful people. It is an endlessly indulgent society. The book's comments regarding ships and sea trade as a tool of wealth acquisition have a particularly Roman accent, for the sea was critical to Roman trade (e.g., Rev 8:9; 18:17b–19). When Babylon falls, distraught merchants cannot find buyers for their "cargo of gold, silver, jewels and pearls, fine linen, purple, silk and scarlet, all kinds of scented wood, all articles of ivory, all articles of costly wood, bronze, iron, and marble, cinnamon, spice, incense, myrrh, frankincense, wine, olive oil, choice flour and wheat, cattle and sheep, horses and chariots, slaves—and human lives" (Rev 18:12–13). They can no longer grow rich on dealing luxury goods and trafficking "human lives." Similarly, Rome's decadent exterior conceals the internal corruption that treats people as commodities: Babylon wears beautiful clothing and jewelry, but when one looks inside of her golden goblet, it is filled with impurity and blood (Rev 17:4–6). Gorgeous and enticing on the outside, the empire is a monster up close. Revelation devotes itself to unveiling the true face of imperial hypocrisy.

The book also associates the empire and its threats to Christian communities with the dangers posed by lies and false teaching. The beast whose number is 666 embodies the lies of the empire and Satan's agents (Rev 13:18). In every way, the sixes in this infamous number fall short of the divine and perfect number seven, just as the beast falls short of the dominant creature it pretends to be. Whether Revelation speaks of 666 to refer to Nero or also to any other false god, the number divulges that the beast is a fake and certainly not God's equal.

When it comes to false teachings in a different setting, namely in the ways that Christian communities conduct themselves, Revelation characterizes falsehoods as much more than simple differences of opinion. Divergent teachings go hand in hand with idolatry, according to Revelation and additional New Testament writings (e.g., Rom 1:22–25; 1 Cor 12:2; 2 Pet 2; 1 John 5:21; Jude 4). In John's visions a false prophet accompanies and supports one of the beasts (Rev 16:13, 19:20, 20:10). Revelation also warns about false teachers influencing the churches of Asia. The book's names for two of them, Jezebel (Rev 2:20; cf. 1 Kgs 16:31; 18:1–19:3; 21:1–24; 2 Kgs 9:22) and Balaam (Rev 2:14; cf. Num 22:1–40; 31:1–20; 2 Pet 2:15–16; Jude 11), recall scriptural stories. The original Jezebel and Balaam were people from outside of ancient Israel whose commitments to foreign gods did great damage to Israel's well-being. When Revelation's messages to Pergamum and Thyatira recall those notorious figures and refer to "fornication" and eating "food sacrificed to idols," the book evidently asserts that the threat of idolatry was not only outside of the church. Possibly some believers in Asia were actively involved in aspects of Roman religion, including emperor worship, and they considered those practices acceptable or within the canopy of Christian freedom. Perhaps their associations with Roman religious values were much more inconspicuous, as simple as forging close social bonds with neighbors who worshiped other deities. Whatever the precise activities targeted for criticism, Revelation veers toward condemning anything that smacks of idolatry. In that regard the book's objections offer a contrast to instructions in Paul's letters (Rom 14:1–15:13, 1 Cor 8:1–11:1). Paul was much more willing to see dietary choices as discretionary and not inescapably harmful to a believer's religious loyalties. Revelation, for its part, calls churches to a sharp sense of differentiation from the religious practices that characterized daily life in their cities and marketplaces.

In addition to all of the criticisms the book directs toward empire, its abuses, and idolatry, Revelation devotes much energy toward explaining what will happen "soon" and toward anticipating final judgment and the emergence of God's new society. The emphasis on urgency and expectation often leads interpreters to assume the book's primary message to its original readers was an appeal for patience mixed with eager and faithful anticipation. But that view overlooks the ways in which the book also urges its audience to separate itself from the dangers and abominations around them. Revelation exposes the monstrosities and hypocrisies of evil and the Roman Empire so that ancient Christ-followers would be equipped to respond.

Revelation exhorts its audience toward defiance instead of passivity and toward resistance instead of compromise. The book does not advocate church-sponsored violence against the empire and its representatives. Neither does it tell Christ-followers to move outside of Rome's boundaries, as if relocating was even economically feasible or escaping the reach of an empire's influence could ever be fully possible. The book does, however, exhort believers to dissociate themselves from Roman values and imperial abuses. Promises to those in the churches who faithfully "conquer" have been examined. Another example occurs when Babylon falls and a voice from heaven says, "Come out of her, my people, so that you do not take part in her sins, and so that you do not share in her plagues" (Rev 18:4).

On one hand, the move to "come out" of Babylon could look as simple as keeping away from temples dedicated to Greco-Roman deities or avoiding certain religious rituals that declared one's allegiance to Rome and endorsed the empire's religiously themed propaganda. But the book's comments about not sharing in Babylon's "sins" and "plagues" suggest that the wider range of Revelation's criticisms of Rome also inform the instructions the book issues to Christ-followers. God's people are urged to disentangle themselves from the empire's sins. Obviously there would have been limits to how much a community of believers in Roman-controlled Asia could have reasonably disavowed participating in political, social, and economic life. The details of this dissociation are less important to Revelation than is the idea of fostering a stronger association with Christ. The book calls for an unyielding loyalty to Christ that manifests itself in actively resisting the empire's idolatrous opulence, exploitations, and lies. The church is not asked to overthrow empires or inflict punishment on imperial powers, for those judgments are only God's work, according to Revelation. At the very least, however, the book makes an appeal to churches to renounce their complacency and focus their attention on the one thing that mattered and the one thing that they could control: bearing witness about Christ in the midst of a system that would undoubtedly not respond kindly to that witness. The goal of doing so is not to provoke, but to reveal. For when the system reacts negatively to the Christian witness, the empire further exposes itself as evil and a false representation of what God truly intends for humanity (e.g., Rev 6:9; 12:17; 13:7–8; 17:6).

Women, Sexuality, and Violence

No New Testament book imagines violence against female bodies as graphically as Revelation does. The book has little to say about actual women in its audience and in the audience's wider context, and nothing to say about how discipleship among women in the churches of Asia might have had distinctive challenges and opportunities in comparison to discipleship among men. Revelation does, however, depict certain symbolic figures as women. The most visible of these figures is Babylon, "the great whore," whose power and centralizing influence are highlighted largely in sexual terms. Similarly, part of Babylon's destruction involves others who humiliate and desecrate—and even consume—the central source of her power over others, which is her body. The people and the beast who hate Babylon "will make her desolate and naked; they will devour her flesh and burn her up with fire" (Rev 17:16). The prophetic language may be ambiguous and symbolic, and it clearly means to refer to the pillaging of a conquered city. The rhetoric sustaining the metaphor of the woman's downfall nevertheless conjures images of real interpersonal violence, including rape, human sacrifice, and cannibalism (cf. Judg 19; Ezek 16:35–41, 23:22–35; Hos 2:2–15; Nah 3:4–6). Similarly problematic language applies to Jezebel, a false teacher in Thyatira (Rev 2:20–23). Her promised comeuppance for her "fornication" involves being thrown "on a bed" (Rev 2:22)—perhaps a reference to exposing her as the immoral person the author says she is, but using an expression that easily conjures images of rape in the minds of readers.

Not only does Revelation liken the defeat of evil and falsehood to the destruction and violation of women's bodies, more generally the book also contrasts purity and profanity in sexual terms. For example, a prostitute serves as the chief symbol of blasphemous abominations. The new Jerusalem, a city of purity and health, appears "as a bride adorned for her husband" (Rev 21:2). The dichotomy between sluts and virgins, with apparently no options in between, deserves criticism. Feeding and further corrupting all this imagery, the book appears to operate with an underlying inability to imagine women and female bodies in ways beyond sexual utility.

Female beings in Revelation ultimately serve to define *men*, either by defiling them or, through the absence of women, by valorizing male purity, as seen in the 144,000 redeemed men who stand with the Lamb on Mount Zion (Rev 14:1–5). That multitude of "blameless" men are described as virgins "who have not defiled themselves with women" (Rev 14:4–5). At the same time, the book does hold up marriage as a positive symbol for the union between Christ and the church (Rev 19:7, 21:2).

The woman clothed with the sun (Rev 12) provides a different kind of female representation, one who possesses some value in and of herself. She gives birth to God's Messiah and to other children of God, probably symbolizing believers. Revelation expresses interest in her as a mother; her sexuality thus comes into focus through her function in childbirth. Nevertheless, precisely as a mother she plays an important role in God's purposes, even though she does not speak and does not appear elsewhere in John's visions. The book's depiction of the woman resonates with various ancient myths about a divine mother. Subsequent Christian interpreters have associated this figure with the Virgin Mary, particularly in imagery associated with the Virgin of Guadalupe. At the very least, the lustrous woman in Revelation symbolizes the cosmic struggle as a struggle between life and death, or between creation and destruction. Revelation may present her even as representative of divine aspects, as a birthing and nurturing life force. Revelation shows respect for her role in fostering God's purposes, although her ongoing existence is largely defined by being on the run from Satan the dragon and needing protection.

Political satire is usually designed to be shocking; its power to denounce often derives from its use of extreme and potentially offensive caricatures. That certainly is true with respect to Revelation. The book does not allow female symbolism to break free from common—and usually damaging—stereotypes. But the book's female imagery remains especially disturbing, on the whole, because the book appears to employ the imagery in such one-dimensional ways. The book never adequately denounces the kind of sexual violence it appears to relish in the most notorious passages. Revelation's visionary rhetoric does not see another side; it hardly challenges its own caricatures. Evidently unaware of the irony, Revelation exploits women and women's sexuality as part of an overriding effort to condemn imperial exploitations.

Those symbolic tendencies of Revelation create problems for anyone who would search for biblical imagery to provide helpful characterizations of evil, falsehood, faithfulness, and sexuality. The same is true for those interpreters who seek from Revelation a strong biblical affirmation of women's value among the people of God. The book's symbols need to be recognized for what they are, as pieces of Revelation's distinctive theological rhetoric: extreme, usually satirical, deliberately polarized, and deeply influenced by patriarchal values. While patriarchal influences show themselves also in other New Testament writings, several of those writings at least illuminate the potential for cracks to weaken patriarchy's stern facades better than Revelation does.

Interpretations of Revelation throughout History

No New Testament book has influenced how Christians understand themselves as participants in an unfolding history toward the arrival of God's ultimate intentions more than Revelation has. Revelation has served as dry kindling in the hands of Christians who want to inflame culture wars with false fantasies of a perpetually persecuted church. It has led some Christians to view the planet and its resources as things to be used up without regret or concern about sustainability, since they believe this world is bound to perish and be remade. For others, Revelation discloses who and how many will really be saved. Interpretations of the book have for centuries fueled separatist movements and "end times" forecasters who are convinced that Revelation's visions and symbols align with the calendar or offer a glimpse into what is really occurring behind specific events in the current news cycle. Some interpreters try to merge the ambiguities of Revelation with other cryptic passages or terms found elsewhere in the Bible. Those mergers often identify the beast from the earth (Rev 13:11–18) with the antichrist named in the Johannine Letters (1 John 2:18, 22; 4:3; 2 John 7) or the lawless one in 2 Thess 2:3, 8. Others insist that Paul's description of Christ's *parousia* in 1 Thess 4:13–18 can align with Revelation's descriptions of judgment and a thousand-year reign (Rev 20). Those kinds of intracanonical mixing and matching, in the end, refuse to respect each individual writing's own distinctive perspective. They appear driven by an insatiable desire to make the Bible into a tool for foretelling the future, instead of by serious attempts to read the books in light of their historical and theological contexts.

The bizarre features of Revelation and the poetic qualities of its rhetoric inspire a wide variety of interpretations and lead some readers to dismiss the book out of hand as a useless relic from an ancient cosmology and a problematic expression of unenlightened ethics. Those features of Revelation nevertheless reiterate a basic theological point that is easier to accept: God remains mysterious, and human beings cannot claim to perceive divine intentions with full clarity. Revelation says the details of God's purposes remain elusive, even after a prophet receives an opportunity to peer into heaven and write about his visions. John does not offer his revelations and symbols as secrets to be decoded, as if each detail has an exact referent in history or corresponds to an entry in an encyclopedia of symbolism. The book's visions are a poetic, evocative attempt to draw believers into an alternate reality, one in which the truly horrifying face of evil becomes readily apparent, but also apparent are God's power and determination to do away with evil and to create something new. Perceiving that basic reality, even with all the mysterious ambiguity, can lead to transformative effects. Having glimpsed the alternate reality and allowing it to inform life in the present world, those who bore witness to Jesus presumably learned from Revelation how imperative and difficult their task was. The book insists that faithful witness can never be easy and may not appear sensible to those outside the church, but bearing witness is the one thing the church can do, in any circumstances, to stand against the idolatries of its day.

Revelation's historical setting cannot be ignored. The original audiences almost certainly did not understand each image in John's literary creation to refer to a certain, specific thing or person. Poetry and symbolism rarely behave in such orderly ways. At the same time, the book's rhetoric remains located in and richly informed by a particular time and place in the late first century CE, and to promote its theological outlook, it draws on Jewish history, experiences, and Scriptures that led up to that time and place. For interpreters today there is great value in focusing on how the book once spoke about an actual empire to actual Christ-followers living in a Roman province. Attention to Revelation's original historical context should not deny, however, that interpreters who have grappled with this book in the midst of various historical and political circumstances have repeatedly found it helpful for unmasking other imperial pretensions, for Revelation's depictions of power dynamics and suffering innocents can find themselves replicated in many forms of imperial abuse. Rome figures prominently in Revelation's evocative rhetoric; but interpreters might see more in Revelation's Rome. One might also consider Rome as representative of other empires and systems. The power of Revelation's insights into the nature of faithfulness and the abusive character of idolatry and oppression has imparted a timeless quality to the book's message.

In recent times Revelation gave lyrics to slave spirituals in America and courage to anti-apartheid movements in South Africa. Today, some interpreters look to Revelation to provide language to characterize pending ecological catastrophe and motivation to protect the earth as a source of divine blessing. As generations come and go, empires and imperial abuses differ in their details, but empires' core attributes of idolatry, pride, and rapaciousness may not be so unusual. Revelation continues to reveal the world's horrors to those interpreters with eyes to see them. Babylon and the beasts can symbolize more than geopolitical empires in general and Rome in particular, just as the oracles of ancient Israel's and Judah's prophets have been heard to rail against new forms of godlessness and injustice across the centuries. Revelation's symbolism has proved itself useful through history in exposing and criticizing any kind of institution that uses people as disposable resources to ensure its own survival and to magnify its own sense of self-importance. Sometimes those institutions lord their power over the church and its people; sometimes they tempt the church and its people to become participants themselves as imperialistic allies and apologists. No one can presume to be immune to the pitfalls, according to John's visions.

When Revelation denounces idolatrous uses of power, whether the offender exposed is a government, a society, a consumer culture, an industry, or even a religious institution, Revelation calls believers to separate themselves and to find constructive power and healing comfort in a slaughtered lamb. Reading Revelation with one eye on the book's historical origins and another eye on the book's capacity to describe an alternate reality made possible by God might encourage the church to avoid the inclination to imitate the kinds of empires that Revelation detests. Because the heart of Revelation's vision of that new reality is a conviction about a powerful God who becomes manifest in the powerlessness of a slaughtered lamb, the book encourages its readers with an argument that is primarily theological—not moral, ethical, or political. As the final book in the New Testament perennially offers new audiences reassurance about a future God will bring into being and motivation to bear witness in the present, Revelation retains its potential to do what it has always aimed to do: to tell Christ-followers who they are and whose they are.

Recommended Resources for Ongoing Exploration of the New Testament

Since there is always more to see in the New Testament, interpreters return to it again and again. Rereading the New Testament itself is only part of the work. Learning from other interpreters along the way is essential for acquiring knowledge, sharpening insight, and joining the lively conversations that biblical interpretations provoke. The following materials provide more detail about the New Testament and its ancient contexts than this companion can. They will help readers conduct deeper investigations of each New Testament writing and related subject matter. For convenience's sake, the list is compact and limited to books, especially those that are well suited for students and others who are relatively new to in-depth study of the New Testament. Only a few of these books are expressly technical analyses. Although the bibliography extends across the entire New Testament—and not just the writings covered in this volume—it is hardly exhaustive or able to represent the full range of opinions concerning interpretive methods and specific debates.

The New Testament's History and Cultural Setting

Adams, Samuel L. *Social and Economic Life in Second Temple Judea*. Louisville, Ky.: Westminster John Knox, 2014.

Carey, Greg. *Apocalyptic Literature in the New Testament*. Core Biblical Studies. Nashville: Abingdon, 2016.

Carter, Warren. *The Roman Empire and the New Testament: An Essential Guide*. Nashville: Abingdon, 2006.

Cohen, Shaye J. D. *From the Maccabees to the Mishnah*. 3rd ed. Louisville, Ky.: Westminster John Knox, 2014.

Collins, John J., and Daniel C. Harlow, eds. *The Eerdmans Dictionary of Early Judaism*. Grand Rapids: Eerdmans, 2010.

Conway, Colleen M. *Behold the Man: Jesus and Greco-Roman Masculinity*. New York: Oxford University Press, 2008.

D'Ambra, Eve. *Roman Women*. Cambridge Introduction to Roman Civilization. New York: Cambridge University Press, 2007.

Freyne, Seán. *The Jesus Movement and Its Expansion: Meaning and Mission*. Grand Rapids: Eerdmans, 2014.

Gamble, Harry Y. *The New Testament Canon: Its Making and Meaning*. Guides to Biblical Scholarship. Philadelphia: Fortress, 1985.

Garnsey, Peter, and Richard Saller. *The Roman Empire: Economy, Society and Culture*. Berkeley: University of California Press, 1987.

Glancy, Jennifer A. *Slavery in Early Christianity*. New York: Oxford University Press, 2002.

Goodman, Martin. *The Ruling Class of Judaea: The Origins of the Jewish Revolt against Rome, A.D. 66–70*. Cambridge: Cambridge University Press, 1987.

Hezser, Catherine, ed. *The Oxford Handbook of Jewish Daily Life in Roman Palestine*. New York: Oxford University Press, 2010.

Hurtado, Larry W. *Destroyer of the gods: Early Christian Distinctiveness in the Roman World*. Waco, Tex.: Baylor University Press, 2016.

Kraemer, Ross Shepard. *Maenads, Martyrs, Matrons, Monastics: A Sourcebook on Women's Religions in the Greco-Roman World*. Philadelphia: Fortress, 1988.

Kraemer, Ross Shepard, and Mary Rose D'Angelo, eds. *Women and Christian Origins*. New York: Oxford University Press, 1999.

Kugel, James L., and Rowan A. Greer. *Early Biblical Interpretation*. Library of Early Christianity 3. Philadelphia: Westminster, 1986.

Law, Timothy Michael. *When God Spoke Greek: The Septuagint and the Making of the Christian Bible*. New York: Oxford University Press, 2013.

MacDonald, Margaret Y. *The Power of Children: The Construction of Christian Families in the Greco-Roman World*. Waco, Tex.: Baylor University Press, 2014.

Magness, Jodi. *Stone and Dung, Oil and Spit: Jewish Daily Life in the Time of Jesus*. Grand Rapids: Eerdmans, 2011.

McDonald, Lee Martin, and James A. Sanders, eds. *The Canon Debate*. Peabody, Mass.: Hendrickson, 2002.

Meyers, Eric M., and Mark A. Chancey. *Alexander to Constantine: Archaeology of the Land of the Bible*. Anchor Yale Bible Reference Library. New Haven, Conn.: Yale University Press, 2012.

Moyise, Steve. *The Old Testament in the New: An Introduction*. 2nd ed. T&T Clark Approaches to Biblical Studies. New York: Bloomsbury T&T Clark, 2015.

Sanders, E. P. *Judaism: Practice and Belief, 63 BCE–66 CE*. Philadelphia: Trinity International, 1992.

VanderKam, James C. *The Dead Sea Scrolls Today*. 2nd ed. Grand Rapids: Eerdmans, 2010.

Vermes, Geza. *The True Herod*. New York: Bloomsbury T&T Clark, 2014.

Jesus, the Gospels, and the Acts of the Apostles

Allison, Dale C., Jr. *The Historical Christ and the Theological Jesus*. Grand Rapids: Eerdmans, 2009.

Brown, Raymond E. *The Birth of the Messiah: A Commentary on the Infancy Narratives in Matthew and Luke*. Anchor Bible Reference Library. New York: Doubleday, 1993.

———. *The Death of the Messiah: From Gethsemane to the Grave: A Commentary on the Passion Narratives in the Four Gospels*. 2 vols. Anchor Bible Reference Library. New York: Doubleday, 1994.

Burridge, Richard A. *What Are the Gospels? A Comparison with Graeco-Roman Biography*. 2nd ed. Grand Rapids: Eerdmans, 2004.

Ehrman, Bart D. *Did Jesus Exist? The Historical Argument for Jesus of Nazareth*. New York: HarperOne, 2012.

Fredriksen, Paula. *From Jesus to Christ: The Origins of the New Testament Images of Christ*. 2nd ed. New Haven, Conn.: Yale University Press, 1988.

Keck, Leander E. *Who Is Jesus? History in Perfect Tense*. Studies on Personalities of the New Testament. Columbia: University of South Carolina Press, 2000.

Keith, Chris, and Larry W. Hurtado, eds. *Jesus among Friends and Enemies: A Historical and Literary Introduction to Jesus in the Gospels*. Grand Rapids: Baker Academic, 2011.

Kloppenborg, John S. *Q, the Earliest Gospel: An Introduction to the Original Stories and Sayings of Jesus*. Louisville, Ky.: Westminster John Knox, 2008.

Le Donne, Anthony. *Historical Jesus: What Can We Know and How Can We Know It?* Grand Rapids: Eerdmans, 2011.

Levine, Amy-Jill. *The Misunderstood Jew: The Church and the Scandal of the Jewish Jesus*. San Francisco: HarperSanFrancisco, 2006.

———. *Short Stories by Jesus: The Enigmatic Parables of a Controversial Rabbi*. New York: HarperOne, 2014.

Perkins, Pheme. *Introduction to the Synoptic Gospels*. Grand Rapids: Eerdmans, 2007.

Sanders, E. P., and Margaret Davies. *Studying the Synoptic Gospels*. Philadelphia: Trinity International, 1989.

Matthew

Boring, M. Eugene. "The Gospel of Matthew: Introduction, Commentary, and Reflections." Pages 87–505 in vol. 8 of *The New Interpreter's Bible*. Edited by Leander E. Keck et al. Nashville: Abingdon, 1995.

Carter, Warren. *Matthew and the Margins: A Sociopolitical and Religious Reading*. Maryknoll, N.Y.: Orbis, 2000.

Overman, J. Andrew. *Church and Community in Crisis: The Gospel according to Matthew*. The New Testament in Context. Valley Forge, Pa.: Trinity International, 1996.

Saldarini, Anthony J. *Matthew's Christian-Jewish Community*. Chicago Studies in the History of Judaism. Chicago: University of Chicago Press, 1994.

Senior, Donald. *Matthew*. Abingdon New Testament Commentaries. Nashville: Abingdon, 1998.

Mark

Byrne, Brendan. *A Costly Freedom: A Theological Reading of Mark's Gospel*. Collegeville, Minn.: Liturgical, 2008.

Dowd, Sharyn. *Reading Mark: A Literary and Theological Commentary on the Second Gospel*. Reading the New Testament. Macon, Ga.: Smyth & Helwys, 2000.

Hooker, Morna D. *The Gospel according to Saint Mark*. Black's New Testament Commentaries. Peabody, Mass.: Hendrickson, 1991.

Malbon, Elizabeth Struthers. *In the Company of Jesus: Characters in Mark's Gospel*. Louisville, Ky.: Westminster John Knox, 2000.

Marcus, Joel. *Mark: A New Translation with Introduction and Commentary*. 2 vols. Anchor Yale Bible. New Haven, Conn.: Yale University Press, 2000–2009.

Myers, Ched. *Binding the Strong Man: A Political Reading of Mark's Story of Jesus*. Maryknoll, N.Y.: Orbis, 1988.

Luke

Carroll, John T. *Luke: A Commentary*. Louisville, Ky.: Westminster John Knox, 2012.

González, Justo L. *Luke*. Belief: A Theological Commentary on the Bible. Louisville, Ky.: Westminster John Knox, 2010.

Green, Joel B. *The Gospel of Luke*. New International Commentary on the New Testament. Grand Rapids: Eerdmans, 1997.

Parsons, Mikeal C. *Luke: Storyteller, Interpreter, Evangelist*. Peabody, Mass.: Hendrickson, 2007.

Ringe, Sharon H. *Luke*. Westminster Bible Companion. Louisville, Ky.: Westminster John Knox, 1995.

Seim, Turid Karlsen. *The Double Message: Patterns of Gender in Luke and Acts*. Nashville: Abingdon, 1994.

John

Bauckham, Richard. *Gospel of Glory: Major Themes in Johannine Theology*. Grand Rapids: Baker Academic, 2015.

Carter, Warren. *John: Storyteller, Interpreter, Evangelist*. Peabody, Mass.: Hendrickson, 2006.

Koester, Craig R. *The Word of Life: A Theology of John's Gospel*. Grand Rapids: Eerdmans, 2008.

Moloney, Francis J. *Love in the Gospel of John: An Exegetical, Theological, and Literary Study*. Grand Rapids: Baker Academic, 2013.

O'Day, Gail R. "The Gospel of John: Introduction, Commentary, and Reflections." Pages 491–865 in vol. 9 of *The New Interpreter's Bible*. Edited by Leander E. Keck et al. Nashville: Abingdon, 1995.

Schneiders, Sandra M. *Written That You May Believe: Encountering Jesus in the Fourth Gospel*. Rev. ed. New York: Herder & Herder, 2003.

Thompson, Marianne Meye. *John: A Commentary*. New Testament Library. Louisville, Ky.: Westminster John Knox, 2015.

Acts

Chance, J. Bradley. *Acts*. Smyth & Helwys Bible Commentary. Macon, Ga.: Smyth & Helwys, 2007.

Gaventa, Beverly Roberts. *Acts*. Abingdon New Testament Commentaries. Nashville: Abingdon, 2003.

Jennings, Willie James. *Acts*. Belief: A Theological Commentary on the Bible. Louisville, Ky.: Westminster John Knox, 2017.

Johnson, Luke Timothy. *The Acts of the Apostles*. Sacra pagina 5. Collegeville, Minn.: Liturgical, 1992.

Skinner, Matthew L. *Intrusive God, Disruptive Gospel: Encountering the Divine in the Book of Acts*. Grand Rapids: Brazos, 2015.

Spencer, F. Scott. *Journeying through Acts: A Literary-Cultural Reading*. Peabody, Mass.: Hendrickson, 2004.

Tannehill, Robert C. *The Narrative Unity of Luke-Acts: A Literary Interpretation*. Vol. 2, *The Acts of the Apostles*. Minneapolis: Fortress, 1990.

Paul and the Pauline Letters

Bassler, Jouette M. *Navigating Paul: An Introduction to Key Theological Concepts*. Louisville, Ky.: Westminster John Knox, 2007.

Beker, J. Christiaan. *Paul the Apostle: The Triumph of God in Life and Thought*. Philadelphia: Fortress, 1980.

Cousar, Charles B. *The Letters of Paul*. Interpreting Biblical Texts. Nashville: Abingdon, 1996.

Horrell, David G. *An Introduction to the Study of Paul*. 3rd ed. T&T Clark Approaches to Biblical Studies. New York: Bloomsbury T&T Clark, 2015.

Meeks, Wayne A. *The First Urban Christians: The Social World of the Apostle Paul*. 2nd ed. New Haven, Conn.: Yale University Press, 2003.

Polaski, Sandra Hack. *A Feminist Introduction to Paul*. St. Louis: Chalice, 2005.

Roetzel, Calvin J. *Paul: The Man and the Myth*. Personalities of the New Testament. Minneapolis: Fortress, 1997.

Ruden, Sarah. *Paul among the People: The Apostle Reinterpreted and Reimagined in His Own Time*. New York: Pantheon, 2010.

Stowers, Stanley K. *Letter Writing in Greco-Roman Antiquity*. Library of Early Christianity 5. Philadelphia: Westminster, 1986.

Romans

Byrne, Brendan. *Romans*. Sacra pagina 6. Collegeville, Minn.: Liturgical, 1996.

Gaventa, Beverly Roberts. *When in Romans: An Invitation to Linger with the Gospel according to Paul*. Grand Rapids: Baker Academic, 2016.

Grieb, A. Katherine. *The Story of Romans: A Narrative Defense of God's Righteousness*. Louisville, Ky.: Westminster John Knox, 2002.

Johnson, Luke Timothy. *Romans: A Literary and Theological Commentary.* New York: Crossroad, 1997.

Keck, Leander E. *Romans.* Abingdon New Testament Commentaries. Nashville: Abingdon, 2005.

Lampe, Peter. *From Paul to Valentinus: Christians at Rome in the First Two Centuries.* Edited by Marshall D. Johnson. Translated by Michael Steinhauser. Minneapolis: Fortress, 2003.

First Corinthians

Fee, Gordon D. *The First Epistle to the Corinthians.* New International Commentary on the New Testament. Grand Rapids: Eerdmans, 1987.

Hays, Richard B. *First Corinthians.* Interpretation. Louisville, Ky.: John Knox, 1997.

Keener, Craig S. *1–2 Corinthians.* New Cambridge Bible Commentary. New York: Cambridge University Press, 2005.

Sampley, J. Paul. "The First Letter to the Corinthians: Introduction, Commentary, and Reflections." Pages 771–1003 in vol. 10 of *The New Interpreter's Bible.* Edited by Leander E. Keck et al. Nashville: Abingdon, 2002.

Wire, Antoinette Clark. *The Corinthian Women Prophets: A Reconstruction through Paul's Rhetoric.* Minneapolis: Fortress, 1990.

Second Corinthians

Collins, Raymond F. *Second Corinthians.* Paideia. Grand Rapids: Baker Academic, 2013.

Matera, Frank J. *II Corinthians: A Commentary.* New Testament Library. Louisville, Ky.: Westminster John Knox, 2003.

Roetzel, Calvin J. *2 Corinthians.* Abingdon New Testament Commentaries. Nashville: Abingdon, 2007.

Sampley, J. Paul. "The Second Letter to the Corinthians: Introduction, Commentary, and Reflections." Pages 1–180 in vol. 11 of *The New Interpreter's Bible.* Edited by Leander E. Keck et al. Nashville: Abingdon, 2000.

Wan, Sze-kar. *Power in Weakness: The Second Letter of Paul to the Corinthians.* The New Testament in Context. Harrisburg, Pa.: Trinity International, 2000.

Galatians

Braxton, Brad Ronnell. *No Longer Slaves: Galatians and African American Experience.* Collegeville, Minn.: Liturgical, 2002.

De Boer, Martinus C. *Galatians: A Commentary.* New Testament Library. Louisville, Ky.: Westminster John Knox, 2011.
Eastman, Susan. *Recovering Paul's Mother Tongue: Language and Theology in Galatians.* Grand Rapids: Eerdmans, 2007.
Hays, Richard B. "The Letter to the Galatians: Introduction, Commentary, and Reflections." Pages 181–348 in vol. 11 of *The New Interpreter's Bible.* Edited by Leander E. Keck et al. Nashville: Abingdon, 2000.
Williams, Sam K. *Galatians.* Abingdon New Testament Commentaries. Nashville: Abingdon, 1997.

Ephesians

Best, Ernest. *Ephesians: A Shorter Commentary.* London: T&T Clark, 2003.
Fowl, Stephen E. *Ephesians: An Introduction and Study Guide: Being a Christian, at Home and in the Cosmos.* T&T Clark Study Guides to the New Testament. London: Bloomsbury T&T Clark, 2017.
MacDonald, Margaret Y. *Colossians and Ephesians.* Sacra pagina 17. Collegeville, Minn.: Liturgical, 2000.
Maier, Harry O. *Picturing Paul in Empire: Imperial Image, Text and Persuasion in Colossians, Ephesians and the Pastoral Epistles.* London: Bloomsbury T&T Clark, 2013.
Perkins, Pheme. "The Letter to the Ephesians: Introduction, Commentary, and Reflections." Pages 349–466 in vol. 11 of *The New Interpreter's Bible.* Edited by Leander E. Keck et al. Nashville: Abingdon, 2000.
Thurston, Bonnie. *Reading Colossians, Ephesians, and 2 Thessalonians: A Literary and Theological Commentary.* Reading the New Testament. New York: Crossroad, 1995.

Philippians

Craddock, Fred B. *Philippians.* Interpretation. Atlanta: John Knox, 1985.
Fee, Gordon D. *Paul's Letter to the Philippians.* New International Commentary on the New Testament. Grand Rapids: Eerdmans, 1995.
Hooker, Morna D. "The Letter to the Philippians: Introduction, Commentary, and Reflections." Pages 467–549 in vol. 11 of *The New Interpreter's Bible.* Edited by Leander E. Keck et al. Nashville: Abingdon, 2000.
Osiek, Carolyn. *Philippians, Philemon.* Abingdon Commentary on the New Testament. Nashville: Abingdon, 2000.

Colossians

Barclay, John M. G. *Colossians and Philemon.* New Testament Guides. Sheffield: Sheffield Academic Press, 1997.

Hay, David M. *Colossians.* Abingdon New Testament Commentaries. Nashville: Abingdon, 2000.

Lincoln, Andrew T. "The Letter to the Colossians: Introduction, Commentary, and Reflections." Pages 551–669 in vol. 11 of *The New Interpreter's Bible.* Edited by Leander E. Keck et al. Nashville: Abingdon, 2000.

MacDonald, Margaret Y. *Colossians and Ephesians.* Sacra pagina 17. Collegeville, Minn.: Liturgical, 2000.

Sumney, Jerry L. *Colossians: A Commentary.* New Testament Library. Louisville, Ky.: Westminster John Knox, 2008.

First and Second Thessalonians

Furnish, Victor Paul. *1 Thessalonians, 2 Thessalonians.* Abingdon New Testament Commentaries. Nashville: Abingdon, 2007.

Gaventa, Beverly Roberts. *First and Second Thessalonians.* Interpretation. Louisville, Ky.: John Knox, 1998.

Malherbe, Abraham J. *Paul and the Thessalonians: The Philosophic Tradition of Pastoral Care.* Philadelphia: Fortress, 1987.

Smith, Abraham. "The First Letter to the Thessalonians: Introduction, Commentary, and Reflections." Pages 671–737 in vol. 11 of *The New Interpreter's Bible.* Edited by Leander E. Keck et al. Nashville: Abingdon, 2000.

———. "The Second Letter to the Thessalonians: Introduction, Commentary, and Reflections." Pages 739–72 in vol. 11 of *The New Interpreter's Bible.* Edited by Leander E. Keck et al. Nashville: Abingdon, 2000.

The Pastoral Letters

Bassler, Jouette M. *1 Timothy, 2 Timothy, Titus.* Abingdon New Testament Commentaries. Nashville: Abingdon, 1996.

Collins, Raymond F. *I & II Timothy and Titus: A Commentary.* New Testament Library. Louisville, Ky.: Westminster John Knox, 2002.

Hultgren, Arland J. *1–2 Timothy, Titus.* Augsburg Commentary on the New Testament. Minneapolis: Augsburg, 1984.

Long, Thomas G. *1 & 2 Timothy and Titus.* Belief: A Theological Commentary on the Bible. Louisville, Ky.: Westminster John Knox, 2016.

Young, Frances. *The Theology of the Pastoral Epistles.* New Testament Theology. New York: Cambridge University Press, 1994.

Philemon

Barclay, John M. G. *Colossians and Philemon*. New Testament Guides. Sheffield: Sheffield Academic Press, 1997.
Callahan, Allen Dwight. *Embassy of Onesimus: The Letter of Paul to Philemon*. The New Testament in Context. Valley Forge, Pa.: Trinity International, 1997.
Felder, Cain Hope. "The Letter to Philemon: Introduction, Commentary, and Reflections." Pages 881–905 in vol. 11 of *The New Interpreter's Bible*. Edited by Leander E. Keck et al. Nashville: Abingdon, 2000.
Fitzmyer, Joseph A. *The Letter to Philemon: A New Translation with Introduction and Commentary*. Anchor Bible 34C. New York: Doubleday, 2000.
Osiek, Carolyn. *Philippians, Philemon*. Abingdon Commentary on the New Testament. Nashville: Abingdon, 2000.

Hebrews, the General Letters, and Revelation

Hebrews

Craddock, Fred B. "The Letter to the Hebrews: Introduction, Commentary, and Reflections." Pages 1–173 in vol. 12 of *The New Interpreter's Bible*. Edited by Leander E. Keck et al. Nashville: Abingdon, 1998.
deSilva, David A. *Perseverance in Gratitude: A Socio-Rhetorical Commentary on the Epistle "to the Hebrews."* Grand Rapids: Eerdmans, 2000.
Johnson, Luke Timothy. *Hebrews: A Commentary*. New Testament Library. Louisville, Ky.: Westminster John Knox, 2006.
Koester, Craig R. *Hebrews: A New Translation with Introduction and Commentary*. Anchor Bible 36. New York: Doubleday, 2001.
Long, Thomas G. *Hebrews*. Interpretation. Louisville, Ky.: John Knox, 1997.

James

Aymer, Margaret P. *James: An Introduction and Study Guide: Diaspora Rhetoric of a Friend of God*. T&T Clark Study Guides to the New Testament. London: Bloomsbury T&T Clark, 2017.
Johnson, Luke Timothy. "The Letter of James: Introduction, Commentary, and Reflections." Pages 175–225 in vol. 12 of *The New Interpreter's Bible*. Edited by Leander E. Keck et al. Nashville: Abingdon, 1998.
McKnight, Scot. *The Letter of James*. The New International Commentary on the New Testament. Grand Rapids: Eerdmans, 2011.

Tamez, Elsa. *The Scandalous Message of James: Faith without Works Is Dead.* New York: Crossroad, 1990.

First and Second Peter and Jude

Bartlett, David L. "The First Letter of Peter: Introduction, Commentary, and Reflections." Pages 227–319 in vol. 12 of *The New Interpreter's Bible.* Edited by Leander E. Keck et al. Nashville: Abingdon, 1998.
Bauckham, Richard. *Jude, 2 Peter.* Word Biblical Themes. Dallas: Word, 1990.
Boring, M. Eugene. *1 Peter.* Abingdon New Testament Commentaries. Nashville: Abingdon, 1999.
Donelson, Lewis R. *I & II Peter and Jude: A Commentary.* New Testament Library. Louisville, Ky.: Westminster John Knox, 2010.
Horrell, David G. *1 Peter.* New Testament Guides. New York: T&T Clark, 2008.
Kraftchick, Steven J. *Jude, 2 Peter.* Abingdon New Testament Commentaries. Nashville: Abingdon, 2002.

The Johannine Letters

Black, C. Clifton. "The First, Second, and Third Letters of John: Introduction, Commentary, and Reflections." Pages 363–469 in vol. 12 of *The New Interpreter's Bible.* Edited by Leander E. Keck et al. Nashville: Abingdon, 1998.
Edwards, Ruth B. *The Johannine Epistles.* New Testament Guides. Sheffield: Sheffield Academic Press, 1996.
Kysar, Robert. *I, II, III John.* Augsburg Commentary on the New Testament. Minneapolis: Augsburg, 1986.
Lieu, Judith M. *I, II, & III John: A Commentary.* New Testament Library. Louisville, Ky.: Westminster John Knox, 2008.
Rensberger, David K. *1 John, 2 John, 3 John.* Abingdon New Testament Commentaries. Nashville: Abingdon, 1997.

Revelation

Blount, Brian K. *Can I Get a Witness? Reading Revelation through African American Culture.* Louisville, Ky.: Westminster John Knox, 2005.
———. *Revelation: A Commentary.* New Testament Library. Louisville, Ky.: Westminster John Knox, 2009.

Gorman, Michael J. *Reading Revelation Responsibly: Uncivil Worship and Witness: Following the Lamb into the New Creation.* Eugene, Ore.: Cascade, 2011.

Koester, Craig R. *Revelation and the End of All Things.* Grand Rapids: Eerdmans, 2001.

Rossing, Barbara R. *The Rapture Exposed: The Message of Hope in the Book of Revelation.* Boulder, Colo.: Westview, 2004.

Schüssler Fiorenza, Elisabeth. *Revelation: Vision of a Just World.* Proclamation Commentaries. Minneapolis: Fortress, 1991.

General Studies of the New Testament Writings

Aymer, Margaret, Cynthia Briggs Kittredge, and David A. Sánchez, eds. *Fortress Commentary on the Bible: New Testament.* Minneapolis: Fortress, 2014.

Blount, Brian K., Cain Hope Felder, Clarice Jannette Martin, and Emerson B. Powery, eds. *True to Our Native Land: An African American New Testament Commentary.* Minneapolis: Fortress, 2007.

Freedman, David Noel, et al., eds. *Anchor Bible Dictionary.* 6 vols. New York: Doubleday, 1992.

Horsley, Richard A., ed. *In the Shadow of Empire: Reclaiming the Bible as a History of Faithful Resistance.* Louisville, Ky.: Westminster John Knox, 2008.

Levine, Amy-Jill, and Marc Zvi Brettler, eds. *The Jewish Annotated New Testament.* New York: Oxford University Press, 2011.

Newsom, Carol A., Sharon H. Ringe, and Jacqueline E. Lapsley, eds. *Women's Bible Commentary.* 3rd ed. Louisville, Ky.: Westminster John Knox, 2012.

O'Day, Gail R., and David L. Petersen, eds. *Theological Bible Commentary.* Louisville, Ky.: Westminster John Knox, 2009.

Patte, Daniel, Teresa Okure, and J. Severino Croatto, eds. *Global Bible Commentary.* Nashville: Abingdon, 2004.

Petersen, David L., and Beverly Roberts Gaventa, eds. *The New Interpreter's Bible One-Volume Commentary.* Nashville: Abingdon, 2010.

Sakenfeld, Katharine Doob, et al., eds. *The New Interpreter's Dictionary of the Bible.* 5 vols. Nashville: Abingdon, 2006–2009.

Subject Index